JUST MY LUCK

Jerry Vass

www.vass.com

This book is a work of nonfiction, however, a few names have been changed to protect their identities.

Copyright © 2017, Jerry Vass and Iris Herrin

This book may not be reproduced in whole or in part, in any form or by any means, electronic or mechanical, including photocopying, recording, or by any information storage and retrieval systems, now or hereafter invented, without written permission of the publisher.

All rights reserved under the Pan-American and International Copyright Conventions.

Printed in the United States of America

For information, contact:

VASS Publishing
1093 A1a Beach Blvd, #448,
Saint Augustine, FL 32080
www.vass.com

'Paris Café'
Front cover photograph by Iris Herrin,
'Paris Rain'
Back cover photograph by Jerry Vass
ISBN: 978-0-9629610-9-0
10 9 8 7 6 5 4 3 2

"Lady Luck is an untrustworthy mistress…"
—The Bubba Ram

GULF STREAM

My plan is quite simple. Sail from Ft. Lauderdale to the Bahamas using the northerly flow of the Gulf Stream to boost the boat along; to sort of slingshot across. When the winds are favorable out of the south, it's a romp. Both wind and water help my boat make her way. In the right conditions, even a small boat can make up to ten knots over the bottom. And that is what we, my boat and I, are doing, using everything to the boat's advantage.

A twenty-three-foot plastic lake boat with a retractable centerboard isn't a deep ocean vessel. It is too light, less than a ton; the keel is too small, and that makes the boat tender, hard to hold on course in big waves. She yaws badly when overpowered by too much wind or too much sail; she will lie down to her leeward gunwale, turn into the eye of the wind and hang there. 'In irons' the sailors call it, stopped in the water, her sails flogging noisily.

Now, the rainbow-colored spinnaker bellies out like an oversized brassiere cupping a pendulous breast, tautly pulling me into the largest river in the world. My little sailboat moves quickly, near her hull speed of six knots, toward West End on Grand Bahama Island. I plan a night entrance into the boat channel sixty-five miles away. It has a green light entrance marker that should be easy to find. The sailing guide says so. I am single-handing so I have to trust the sailing guide.

With the wind at my back it is a classic downhill romp out of Ft. Lauderdale. I blow north with the current along the beach, empty in the morning light, too early for yesterday's toasty-red tourists to muster for today's sun wars.

I'll steer away east, get a chart position and draw a course. I roll the tiller slightly and adjust the sheets, easing the lines around the winch heads and cleat them.

A quick Gulf Stream crossing and I will be in the Bahamas where I can duck behind islands out of the rough seas married to powerful winds. And, so far this morning it is going better than planned, although I hadn't expected a southeasterly wind quite this powerful.

As the wind builds slowly and steadily I lower the big bra cup, the thin nylon sliding around on deck until I jam it into its sailbag and drop it down the forward hatch. I replace it with a standard jib since, if the wind is building, I won't have to change again unless it gets rough. In a big wind, changing headsails on this small boat can be life threatening. Even on my buddy Bob Callard's boat that is six times heavier and a real stiff New England deep-water craft, changing a headsail in big wind gets dicey.

I have made this crossing twice on Bob's boat. He is my mentor. He is an engineer and technically well grounded; he has sailed the Great Lakes since he was a kid and has lots of sea time. And he understands everything. I have worked with him to prepare for this cruise and I am sure there are gaps in my knowledge. Sometimes, when teaching, Bob makes poor assumptions about my sailing knowledge. And, like a fool, I let him. When I make mistakes Bob just smiles slyly out of his gray beard. That smile makes me crazy, embarrassing me in my ignorance. To avoid that chiding smile I won't admit my ignorance so I don't learn things I should know.

I sail briskly through the morning. In the early afternoon the wind shifts from the south around to the west across my port beam. That worries me. While it is giving me a lift now what if the wind continues to shift north? If it does, it could be a nasty trip.

I lounge in the cockpit, drink a beer and nibble Cheetos.

This isn't the lakes of Colorado or San Diego Bay. Out here in the deep blue transparent currents of the river in the ocean, I feel like a real sailor, plying the same ocean stream the Spaniards used to ship home blood-soaked Indian gold and silver from the New World: the Spanish Main, a deep and totally impersonal river that is now acting friendly with two-foot swells but in minutes can become a deadly maelstrom. There is no estimating the number of lives the Gulf Stream has stolen. Out here, when you drown, your remains turn to shark turds that float off toward New England, by Newfoundland, south of Greenland, by Ireland and then west of Europe. That's the theory. There is no reason to believe that a drowned body floats more than a few miles before it becomes a shark's sweet and tender breakfast. Only last week a fisherman cut a shark's belly open to find a man's partially digested foot still laced into a new, white Nike running shoe. The sea isn't malevolent by nature; it's simply uncaring, neutral, minding neither cause nor effect. A sailor deals with the sea's changeable personalities as they come. As in few other places on earth a man must take care of himself out here. I like that bargain.

It is nearly dark. Then, out of the northwest, bruised clouds come in low and fast like vaporous fighter planes that strafe the tops off the waves. This is no place to take a knockdown, where a wind gust knocks the boat over, and wind pressure in the sail holds the boat flat. Held down too long, the sea floods the cockpit and then the cabin. Then the boat sinks. Every boat in the world is fighting to get to the bottom. I don't want to help this one.

I shorten the mainsail to the first set of reef points and the small boat stands up straighter, rides better. Her weather-helm, the tiller pressure, eases; she steers better.

The dead reckoning course I've laid out on the chart is an estimate at best. Computing time and distance are easy, but when you add in the big river's wandering current and leeway, the side-slipping of the boat, and the laissez-faire attitude of the sailor, it's impossible to pencil-point a chart and say, "This is my exact location." I have no need for an exact location. An error of three or four miles is close enough for me.

The wind against the current begins to stack the waves into six-foot hillocks that crest, break, fall apart and drop into nothing. The boat bobs onto and then over the white tops, sometimes dropping dramatically into the hole beyond. Each plunge leaves my stomach in the air until it too falls—into a pool of burgeoning nausea.

It is dark, as dark as the real world gets, a blackness unseeable. The boat has only one battery. My weak running lights reflect off the fast, foamy water and occasionally highlight the crest of a wave breaking close aboard.

The compass light glows red; the rolling, wandering, rotating ball perfectly projects the boat's motion in miniature. The red light turns into a smear. Tears. A wave of fear comes over me. I have more than a hint of nausea.

The self-steering rig that I spent hours researching, designing and building out of surgical tubing doesn't work very well. It will keep the vessel on course for a minute, but the boat wanders off when a big puff comes, rounds up into irons and stops.

Sea motion excites the little hairs in the middle ear to a state of erection that is hardwired to the stomach. I steer with my foot as it takes four or five minutes to calculate and draw my estimated position on the chart. In the first minute, my stomach rebels and I toss it all, flash what is left of the Cheetos and beer into the cockpit sole where it mixes with salt water and swirls around my feet, back and forth with each wave like little orange buoys.

By rough estimate, I am twenty miles from West End Bahamas and may be a touch high to the course line. Maybe I ought to steer a little more to the east, maybe even dead east. It is ten o'clock. After sailing twelve hours this means at least another three hours, perhaps longer, before I can rest

I don't see how I can be south of the course. With a twenty-knot wind on my nose and a four-knot current pushing north, I am doing all right. I don't want to stay too far south. It makes Grand Bahama a lee shore. If the wind keeps blowing from the North it will be a lee shore anyway. Sailboats work well if there is plenty of sea room. A lee shore is the sailor's biggest fear, it means being driven up onto the beach by a strong, inexorable, merciless wind and being tumbled in the surf, the boat rolling over and over, dismasting, reduced to a beaten hulk in the rocks and foam. A lee shore makes for a big adventure. I will avoid that.

Around midnight, the waves are falling into themselves from ten feet. The cresting caps break a building story above my little boat, spitting off spray that flies away downwind like parade confetti. My boat slides into the troughs with a shiver and then the wind pressure in her sails decreases, and she stands up, slowly climbs out of the hole and up the next hill only to skid away to the bottom of the next hill. She yields to the growling wind like a featherweight boxer. She is doing fine. Her captain is tired and seasick. Beating around in a tiny boat is like being trapped in a paint mixer.

I try to focus on the chart with the straight pencil line drawn from Ft. Lauderdale to West End. I gag down my nausea. I'm frustrated. I know in my heart the line now means nothing. A real line of my course would look more like a snake's trail in the New Mexico sand heading off to God knows where.

The wind shifts more to the north and pushes up building-sized stacks of water. There is no way to tell where I am.

I start talking to Callard. "I think I'm lost," I say to him aloud. "I think I'm five miles out of West End but, to be honest, I don't know if I am north or south of the entry. I think it's over there somewhere. If it is we should see lights soon."

Callard doesn't answer. For what seems like a long time I peer east into velvet blackness. I'm not sure at first, then a couple of waves later, I am sure. Indeed, there is one tiny flickering light quickly covered by waves.

I yell, "A light, Callard, there's a goddam light."

It could be another boat. But that is unlikely. Only fools like me are caught out in this weather. All the smart sailors are tied up to solid land, drinking gin and tonics and caressing the fannies of beautifully tan, bikini-clad airline stewardesses euphemistically called "crew" in this part of the world.

"Head toward that light." I bark. Just giving a command with confidence makes me feel better. The light grows steadily stronger. "Hey, Callard, that has to be West End. Steer for the light," I say, "then we'll follow the beach to the channel entrance. My man, we've got it made."

Callard smiles broadly, "A hell of a piece of navigation," he says.

I feel great. We have done it. Against wind and wave, Callard and I have sailed across one of the most unpredictable and dangerous stretches of water in the hemisphere and found the port we were looking for. And in a Clorox-bottle boat. I don't mind that he didn't say "Sir." He should have; I am the captain.

The light is hidden from us by the waves. In some minutes, we climb out on top of a wave; the light is nearer. As we close, the light quickly separates into a group of individual lights. I think I can see people moving in front of the lights.

"I think it's a motel," I say. "See the outdoor room lights? It's a beach motel on West End that's what it is. Steer right at it." We seem to be closing in on it fast, faster than usual. Each wave brings us noticeably closer to the motel. It is now large enough that I am scanning to take in the length of it. Somehow, it seems very close; too close too soon.

Then the motel moves. Actually moves. The room lights roll a bit from side to side. I see green and red lights on each end of the motel and a white light way up on the roof. Recognition of death comes sparkling like a ball of St. Elmo's fire. It electrifies my mind and sends a shock to my vocal cords.

I scream over the noise, "It's a ship! It's a big fuckin' ship! It's right on us! Collision! Collision! Tack! Tack!" My voice goes hoarse. The backs of my legs go hot. We are on a collision course. My weak running lights are mostly under water. They can't see us. We have no chance in a collision. We will be flattened like prairie dog road-kill.

"Tack! Goddam it, tack!" I yell to Callard.

I throw the helm over and dive through the hatch. I fumble for the masthead strobe light switch, a bright flasher on the tip of the mast that lights up the waves around us. As we come into the eye of the wind we nearly stop; the jib backs fully and wraps against the mast, the boat heels dangerously over, equipment falling noisily from a storage locker into the cabin sole. With backed sails, the boat is trying hard to sail in a circle. I jump back topside, grab the loose tiller and release the jib sheet. The sail flogs, pops and cracks until I trim it and the boat stands up and regains her footing. Suddenly we are pinpointed in a powerful spotlight. I click on the radio and flip the selector to the ship-to-ship channel.

"Spotlight...this is yacht Street Hustler...over." My voice quivers in the mike, and I hate it.

"Yeeeaaah, Street Hustler, what the hell are you doin'?" His voice sounds stressed through the static, his first word drawn out, almost a yodel.

"We're trying to stay alive. We have reversed course away from you." As we ride high on a wave, the spotlight floods into the cockpit. My fingers squeeze tightly around the teak tiller and I lean forward as if to coax our little craft to go faster.

I think about what Callard would do. Callard wouldn't be lost. Callard is never lost or even confused. He always knows what to do. And he is never afraid. I look around the boat as if there is some solution to my problem I have overlooked. I glance at the chart with the phony straight pencil line. I can see Callard with that goddam grin making fun of me. I swallow hard and click on the mike. "Spotlight...could you give me a magnetic course and distance to West End, please?"

"Yeeeaah. Stand by, Street Hustler..." the radio says. The spotlight goes out and we are in blackness.

The huge ocean-going tug goes by our stern so closely we lift on her bow wave and we hear its diesel exhausts over the raging wind. We look up at her sides and see how steadily she rides with a slow, stately roll. All her crew is dry and warm. We are cold and wet and scared and shaking.

The radio hisses on. "Yeeeaaah...your course to West End is one zero five magnetic, eighteen miles."

"Thank you for your assistance. We really appreciate it." I say as sincerely as I can.

"Yeeeah...Good luck." There is a touch of sarcasm in the skipper's voice.

"Callard, we are way the hell out here. I wonder how we got way the hell out here?"

"I told you to stay south of the course," Callard says without feeling.

I apologize, "It was the lee shore, I wanted to stay away from the lee friggin' shore."

On the chart, I shakily draw a new course line to West End and step off the distance with dividers. My hand wobbles and it takes me three tries to get the dividers to stick into the chart paper. We are twenty miles north of where we should be. I see Callard grin again. It is annoying.

And I see another problem. The narrow channel entrance is open to the north. In this northern blow it is a lee shore with thirty knots or better of wind and crashing surf. We will have minimum control even with bare poles and high boat speed, no way to slow it and no margin for error. If we miss the channel we will most certainly end up rolling in the huge surf and aground. Just to get to the channel entrance we have to navigate a slim gut of a pass a half-mile wide between a small rocky island to the north and Grand Bahama's beach to the south.

Should we go in there? If not, we will have to turn and run south along the big island another three hours to find shelter. A tough prospect. The little boat bobs around on the heavy waves like a light bulb; it beats and abrades my body to raw exhaustion. And I am hung over from the adrenaline rush of the near-death brush with the tug.

What would Callard do? He is in Miami at the dock at Dinner Key, living it up, looking cool and tan and salty, sitting on the fantail of his blue-water boat, telling sea stories to the rich yachties who listen, enraptured.

I can hear him telling his story. With a big smile and a far-off look he will lean back holding his glass of vintage white wine and say, "We had the choice of going into this blind pass in a norther or turning south to a nice safe harbor at Freeport, but I decided that we would risk the West End channel." The yachties ooh and aah. Callard shrugs his heavily muscled shoulders and lifts his bushy eyebrows, "Well, you can't live forever..." he says and sips his wine. Nods and big smiles all around.

I take a deep breath. If he can do it so can I. "Okay Callard, let's give it a try. In that pass, there should be enough water to turn around and come out. The entrance to the boat channel is supposed to have a green marker light. If we see the light, we'll sorta sneak up and take a look at the entrance. If it's too dangerous, we'll tack back out."

"Hey, we're doin' great," I say. "I'll just steer between the rocks and the beach, and we'll do fine."

"Whatever you say." Callard doesn't sound convinced.

The new course puts the wind on our beam, an ideal point of sail. The boat settles nicely into the rhythm of sliding down this trough and climbing onto that crest, and I settle back into an easier mood. Digging around, I find some dry crackers to help dampen the nausea. I am too tired to talk. I just steer hunkered down out of the spray, listening to the wind howl in the rigging and the nearby crash of waves as they collapse on themselves.

Entering West End proves to be tight. It is a mean place in a norther.

I decide to drop the jib and go under mainsail only. It reduces our power but handling one sail allows fewer potential foul-ups. Without the jib we can't beat upwind as well, but the boat is more manageable in tight quarters. Dousing the jib means I have to go forward into the leaping, crashing world of water and wildness. I watch for a while to see what kind of wave predictability exists. There isn't any. I set up my self-steering invention and buckle on a safety harness with a lead line.

"Don't go over the side..." Callard whispers "or you'll die, and nobody will ever know."

I crawl up out of the security of the cockpit and inch myself along the high side of the boat. Halfway forward, I snap my safety lead onto a lifeline. The boat pitches high on a wave then plunges down into a black pit, falling weightlessly. I float in the air, clear of the deck. The bow crashes into the water, and I slam down. The spray stings my eyes as it breaks over me. I feel the boat round up slightly. I let go of the jib sheet and then the halyard. The sail flogs wildly, snapping and cracking, the lines flail like wild snakes, the jib's steel shackle whips around trying for my eyes, trying hard to blind me. On my knees, I reach up and frantically pull on the sailcloth, hand over hand, piling it on the deck inside the lifelines. I roll onto the stack of wet nylon and push it up against the lifeline netting. Each time the boat plunges into an abyss the bow wash breaks over me. In a minute, I am exhausted, and my breath is short. Callard's face comes up and says, "You should have done this before it got so dangerous."

I tie off the sail, so it can't be swept overboard in a wave. I crawl back into the cockpit and shiver. Callard grins at me. I steer back to the course and trim the main.

This time the lights of West End are real. They are on the radio tower with red lights at the point of the pass. I confirm it on the chart. As we enter the thin pass, we can see waves breaking ashore: a threatening white line of disaster and death. We enter shallower water and, behind a rocky outcrop, the waves moderate a bit but the wind still howls, screeching in the shrouds.

I keep my eyes peeled to starboard for a green channel light over there on the land.

Callard and I sail tentatively, feeling our way into the pass, the wind drives us deeper into the trap. With each yard of water it is harder to extricate ourselves, and we become more committed to the surf line. And here, close aboard the port side, is a rocky little island to the north, with waves smashing over its black rocks and breaking high, the spray flying far downwind into the pass.

"Can you see anything, Callard? The chart shows that the boat channel is a mile or so in beyond that antenna. We're there, and we're about outta deep water." We strain for a light ashore, any light.

"I can't see any light. I think we ought to get out of here," I say. "We've got white water here and there both." I point from one rocky island to the other. The narrowing pass shows white water even ahead of us. "We should tack while there's still room, still time," I say aloud.

"Nah," Callard says. "We better jibe out, keep the wind behind us. We're on a lee shore. We don't want to lose power in a tack. Watch the boom when it flies over. Jibe-oh-duck!" I push the tiller over with my knee into the turn; the little boat stands up straight as the pressure eases off her centerboard, then the boom swings violently across the cockpit with a crash, the shock vibrating through the boat and resonating in the rigging. Now we are barely outside the combers. Breaking crests mark the line where the incoming waves feel the ground and build height, building until they collapse onto themselves spilling tons of water to the bottom, relentlessly pummeling everything in their reach to destruction.

"Dammit Callard, the wind has shifted a touch. I can't beat away from the beach!"

I sheet in the main sail hard and struggle to get the boat to head up, away from the breaker line. Without the jib, she doesn't respond. It is too late. I look to windward at a wall of water climbing, steepening, darkening, curling, boiling, breaking at the crest, white teeth gnashing viciously above us. Under my breath, I say matter-of-factly, "Hold on, Callard, we're going over."

The big wave slaps the boat hard, black water breaks over her cabin and twists her onto her beam-ends, her mast horizontal, the head nearly touching the water. She surfs sideways down the wave wall. I looked back at the rudder, and it is clear of the water. Now we are out of control, at the mercy of the white-capped breaker sliding us to the rocks, toward a killing impact. I can hear things breaking inside the cabin. I stand mesmerized, my feet on the low side of the cockpit which is taking water, my hands straining the upper lifeline. Saltwater flows over the edge of the cockpit like a dam spillway. I watch the setup for sinking with horrified fascination. I am just a passenger. The boat slides sideways. She trembles down the face of the wave, and it feels like she wants to give up, roll over like a fat woman, and sink. But she hangs there, undecided. Then her keel weight overwhelms her, and she decides not to roll. She lazily stands up, the water sheeting overboard, racing along the toe rail and out of her scuppers. She rounds up into the eye of the wind and shakes herself like a wet dog. Then she falls off the wind and starts sailing again as if nothing has happened, salt water draining out of the cockpit, shedding weight.

The wind shifts back. I can now gain distance on the deadly breaker line. "I thought for a minute we were going for a swim," Callard says in my ear.

"Damn close. Damn close ... " is all I can say. My entire body is shaking.

By pinching the wind, we carefully work our way along a few yards outside the breaker line and around the point into the deep black ocean. Open water never felt so good.

Callard says, "You went in too far, didn't you? You were late on your decision, weren't you? You trusted the Bahamian navigation markers, didn't you?"

"Yeah, Goddam it, I did," I whisper.

"You forgot that for a hundred years the Bahamian people made their living luring ships aground by moving navigation markers then stripping them bare. They call it wracking."

"Yeah, I did. I forgot that," I say.

In the small hours of the morning, inside the Freeport commercial harbor, I tie up opposite a cruise ship at a dock so high one can barely see the tip of Street Hustler's mast from it. I speak to the dock master briefly, as if in a dream, and then I sleep hard and late.

Near noon I stop by the harbormaster to pay my dock fee. Inside his plain little office, the January sun slants across a blackboard with columns drawn on it. The headings are Ship Name/Home Port/Length/Captain.

The first line of chalked words says

'SS Norway-Oslo-1035 feet-Capt. Svensen'

Underneath, the next line says

'SV Street Hustler-Telluride-23 feet-Capt. Vass'.

I stare at my name on the blackboard and chuckle.

Callard's face comes up, his jaw set. He shakes his head. "You're a dangerous man to sail with," he says sadly.

FOSTER HOME

Living in a strange place isn't strange for me. I grew up as a stranger in other people's houses while my father was a federal fugitive, so being boarded out is normal for me. But everyone in this foster home is basically crazy.

Mom and Pop Eliot are Christians, the Holy Roller kind, and they take us all to church three times a week. Mostly I sit there quietly on a folding chair, watching and doubting. Like now, listening to the organ loudly hum its mournful songs, I watch the preacher's wife's foot graze along the foot pedals and her delicate hands float, and land, and park on the keys. Heavy bass notes bounce off the low ceiling and its rows of fluorescent tubes, mounted in lines, that converge at the altar above the sweating preacher. He waves a Bible, his thumb between the pages. It flops around as he waves it like a magic wand above the rapt congregation. His voice rises in excitement, ejaculated spit flickers through the low spotlight coming from the side of the stage; the spotlight is carefully shaded, so that it only shines on him, out of the eyes of the congregants. His pink scalp shows through his thin blonde hair and head-sweat dribbles into his collar. His voice drops to a stage whisper. The worshipers lean forward in their seats, straining to hear every word, every heated syllable, every grunt and labored breath, every sucking in of sweaty air, every rhythmic exhalation, and every violent punctuation.

Near the front, a man begins to speak loudly in a foreign language. I don't understand a word, but 'amens' pop up around the room, one here, then there, as women's voices, trembling with emotion, answer the man down front. After a time, the man's voice stops, and the room falls quiet.

"What'd he say?" I ask Mom.

"Shuuuuh," she says.

Then the preacher says breathlessly, "Praise the Lord, tonight Brother Samuel has been the messenger of our Lord Jesus Christ and spoken to us in tongues."

Amens explode around the crowd like little firecrackers bouncing along the floor.

"The Lord Jesus Christ says this is a blessed congregation." The preacher's arms are outstretched on a phantom cross, his eyes are closed, his quivering hands hover over the people and droplets of perspiration fall through the light onto the carpeted stage. "Jesus is here among us and He blesses us all."

Amens again; Bibles wave in the air. I don't see Jesus anywhere. I must have missed him. How can these people get so excited by something they cannot see?

Driving the ten miles home, there is little talk. The gray Dodge has a constant rattle like a loose muffler. Sleepily, I wonder what the foreign language talk was all about. Was there actually a visit from Jesus Himself? Would he show up in that garage building with concrete floors? I guess it could happen. Everybody seemed convinced and got excited. It was weird. Something happened. Just watching made me feel guilty. But Jesus? Really?

My current home is a lot roomier than my dad's trailer house. Here, I have a skinny bed to myself and a mattress without too many lumps. If I settle in just right, I can avoid most of them. A half dozen kids live in the basement; all of them are crazy and weird, and some are ugly, too but I'm not any of those things; I am regular.

Being out of the reach of my father's fists is a relief. I learned a long time ago to keep a low profile, not look anyone in the eye. When I do, people think it is a challenge to a fight. It isn't, but if it happens it happens, I must fight or my old man will whip me if I don't. He used to be a professional boxer and he taught me how to fight, to hit a guy and hurt him. I don't want to but I will. The Old Man whips my ass if I lose.

He was born in the Appalachian Mountains and trained me to always answer adults with "Yes, Sir" and "No, Sir," and "Yes, Ma'am" and "No, Ma'am," and to never say "Sir" to a black man. Forgetting to do so meant a backhand that he called his "knuckle sandwich." Because I was polite, the neighbor ladies in the trailer park would sometimes fuss over me and embarrass me. Women always make me uncomfortable. I never know how to act around them when they cluck over me.

I've never met my own mother but this foster mom is a good, God-fearing woman. She is motherly and kind, on the fat side with gray hair and flowered print dresses. All her children are grown up and gone except for a prissy son with a college degree. He lives out back over the garage with his stern blonde wife, and a kid daughter. Those folks don't mix with us in the main house, but they come down the stairs and sit at the big family table and eat meals with us. We all politely listen when Mom talks or when Prissy Son holds forth importantly on some subject we don't understand. He doesn't care if we foster kids exist. I said hello to him once, and he just stared at me; not at me, through me.

Weekday mornings I walk the mile to school. Along the railroad track, by the dark OK Rubber Welders plant, then across the Main Street and up the hill to Littleton High School. I sit in the classroom and smell the sack lunches and look out through the windows to the distant mountains. I want to be over there or at least someplace away from here. Anywhere away.

I have plans, plans to buy a car. I'll become a journeyman bricklayer like my old man and make really good money, buy a good car, a used one but a good one; a Mercury maybe that I can soup up, paint candy-apple-red. I'll have a girlfriend that sits very close to me, and we'll cruise main street and I'll drive with one hand high on the steering wheel and keep my arm around her while everybody on the sidewalk watches us go by. I don't talk now unless I have to but, with my own girl, we can talk all we want. She might be my friend. There is a lot I want to tell her.

I don't know anything about girls except that they smell good and giggle a lot and stand around in small groups and laugh and clap their hands and glance sideways at me and whisper.

Boys and girls come and go in the foster home, but some stay—those kids that are in the way or whose parents can't feed them or hate them and want them gone. We live in the basement of this big house; girls sleep in their own room, boys in theirs. Lights go out at ten o'clock. In the winter mornings, lights come on at six. We have oatmeal for breakfast. The table is set without a sugar bowl.

Until lights out, we gather around the big table and play board games or just talk or study or read the Bible. I don't like the Bible. I like books about real people and things like war. The Marine Corps is my favorite subject. I'm going to be a marine when I get out of school; a trained killer and tough enough to fight my old man. One day, when he is beating on me, maybe I'll kill him.

One of the kids is a big guy, older than the rest of us. He has broad shoulders and is light skinned, with deep pockmarks from zits. He is ugly. But nice. The girl of his choice is a dumb kid who is also downright ugly. They do sex. I've seen them. He jacks off a lot. I hear him in the middle of the night.

Sex is foreign to me, something men and women do when they are out of high school, maybe in college. I have sex feelings and touch myself a lot, but I don't tell anyone. It is my secret. My earliest feelings of sex were when my old man returned from the store and caught me rubbing my tiny, hard little finger on the velour seat of the '39 Ford. Maybe I was five. I didn't understand what I felt when he caught me, but I found out later it was called embarrassment.

It is winter and there is a fire in the fireplace, making shadows move on the low ceiling. The nice acne boy and his girl are on the floor, he humps and grunts in the firelight, and her breath comes out in gasps. Against the flickering fire I can only see silhouettes, but I know what they are doing.

I am disturbed by the scene. It hangs in my brain. I wonder what it is like to have a girl let you do that to her? She would have to like you a lot, I guess. I don't think any girl will ever like me enough to let me do that to her. Besides, I'd have to trust her not to tell anyone. I can't do that. You just can't trust people with secrets like that. Or anything else as far as I can tell.

Often, a new kid will come to the basement and live with us and there is always something not quite right about them. Like my new roommate. He's not a roommate actually, but he got the bed next to me in the boy's bedroom. He is always neatly dressed and very protective of his clothes, wiping the slightest spot off his jeans. "I never wash my Levis," he says, and they are always as clean as a china plate. He only has one pair, and he protects them like his skin. At dinner, he covers his pants with a towel. He acts nervous. So weird.

    A new girl just moved into the girl's bedroom. She has dark brown eyes and dishwater blonde hair and bad skin. Very skinny. Dirty dress. This is ordinary since most of the kids come from poor families. Across the big table, at dinner, I watch her carefully, and she catches me staring at her. Her eyes cut away to some distant place and then drop to her plate. She never speaks, always eats quickly and then leaves the table.

    A few days later, as a group, we walk toward school along the railroad track and by the rubber plant. She ends up walking next to me.

    "What's your name?"

    "Mary," she answers in a near whisper.

    "What's your last name?"

    "Hockenberry. I'm Mary Elizbeth Hockeberry," she says defiantly.

    "What are you doing here?" I ask.

    She doesn't look at me. "My Daddy…"

    "What'd he do?"

    "He made me do things…"

    "What things?"

    No answer. We walk on.

    Every kid here has a story. Some are about being beaten up, some about drinking, some about sex. Some are just about hate. But we don't talk about them. We all have some kind of pain from our family lives and an unspoken envy of kids who have normal families: a father, and a mother and brothers and sisters who don't hurt them. We get visits from the county social workers, and we tolerate their attempts to make us feel better, but they have little effect on our internal lives, our haunted thoughts, our hidden fears, our dreads, for we are all good at hiding our terrors of the past, the present, and the future, the lonely, secret knowledge of fists and belts or slaps or sex parts, the gasoline breath of alcohol or probing fingers and hate-filled words, and the isolation of not having a friend in the world, of not belonging anywhere or to anyone who loves us. Like I said, the kids here are all somewhat crazy, but I'm really okay. I'm not one of them.

Wednesday night is Vespers night at the Holy Roller church. On the way back home, Mary and I sit close in the back seat of the Dodge. As it rattles through the dark, her leg sends warm feelings into mine. My hand snakes over her hand. She holds it in her lap, and squeezes it tight. I put my arm around her thin neck and kiss her on the cheek. I smell the oil in her hair. She turns her lips to mine, and we kiss. And then the car turns into the driveway of the home and it is over.

The next day, she is feeding the chickens, alone in the yard, scattering corn from a bucket.

"Hey…" I say.

She looks at me with the touch of a smile. "Hey…"

"How ya doin'?"

"Okay…"

"I liked th' other night in the car," I whisper.

She nods.

"I'd like to do that again."

She looks at me directly and nods.

"What are you doin' out here?"

"Feed'n the chickens and collectin' eggs."

She tips the bucket over, and the last few kernels rattle out to the ground.

"I gotta go get th' eggs," she says, and turns and walks into the hen house.

I follow her. Inside, it smells of chicken droppings, warm and close. She feels around in the straw and carefully places eggs in her bucket.

I step up behind her, slip my arm around her waist, and turn her gently. Her face comes to me, and we kiss and then kiss some more. It is good, and I can feel a familiar feeling in my pants. As we kiss, I move my hand to her breast and squeeze it gently. It is barely a handful. It feels good.

"I can't..." she says, pulling back. Tears well up in her eyes.

She quickly turns and walks away.

I stand in the coop, alone with the smell of chicken poop. Well, all these kids are crazy, I think to myself. I wonder what I did to make her cry. I was just trying to be nice. I thought she liked me.

Right before dinner Mom comes looking for me in the basement. She looks grave. "Come with me. We need to talk," she says.

We go up out of the basement and across the large yard and sit at the picnic table under the half-dead tree. The lights from the house stare like eyes.

There is a long silence, then she hisses "You have to leave."

I am surprised. I like it here, away from my old man. Nobody beats me here.

"Why?"

"Because you molested the girl," she whispers harshly, "You know what you did...you ought to be ashamed of yourself...you have dirty ideas, and you touched her with your dirty hands."

She looks off across the valley to those distant blue mountains and slowly shakes her head.

"Pack your clothes. Your father will come to get you in the morning. Don't...you...show...your...face...back...here...again...ever!"

"Get in the car, boy," the Old Man growls the next morning, in that familiar accusing tone. I slide sideways into the seat and sit tightly against the door to leave the most possible space between me and the knuckle-sandwich. He scowls straight ahead.

We drive. He never asks what happened at the home. Nobody ever did. And I never said. Because I am not crazy.

TYPHOON

I gag down the bile.

The gun director turret, the highest enclosed structure on this warship, is fifty-five feet above the waterline. It rolls heavily in an eighty-degree arc and we sailors inside the cramped, hot space, swallow hard when the bow pitches into a wave-hole that releases gravity and bile rushes up into our throats.

I can't throw up, not trapped in here with Chief Hoover. It would be too humiliating. I am a deep-water sailor, a salt. This ship, my home of three years, is my steel mistress, my loaded gun, my prison, and my duty. I know her wild ways in a storm. But the Chief is a true hero. A shipwreck survivor.

The South China Sea is rough in a typhoon; the waves are several stories deep, with surf that breaks high then tumbles into itself then slides steeply into the next ragged canyon. The ship's sharp bow pitches headlong into the hole with a white crash of spray that turns into black water—it eats the bow and rushes back, washing around the superstructure. She shivers almost to a stop. Then she shakes herself and her bow lifts reluctantly. The dark water spills over her sides in white waterfalls, driven spume flies up and away, arcing across her entire length in the hundred-knot wind, the vibrating violence adding to the constant pitching and heavy rolling from starboard to port and back again. She rolls near the point of capsize.

In a forty-five-degree roll, a ship lives on borrowed time; anything beyond forty-five degrees makes a sailor think of the dry home in Nebraska that he will never see again. A ship is at the mercy of gigantic forces of nature and the competence of the architects that designed it. Since the designers of this boat finished their tank-testing back in landlocked Maryland some twenty years ago, has new heavy equipment been added above the waterline? Has added weight topside changed the center of gravity; changed the righting moment—the ship's need to recover from a roll—to save herself in heavy seas?

When a ship rolls beyond forty-five degrees, it is nearing the bitter end. Typhoons are massive storms, tenacious in their attempts to sink every floating object. When the height of a wave from crest to trough exactly matches the width of the hull, a ship can roll upside down. The beam of my four-hundred-foot ship is thirty-nine feet eight inches. If caught crossways beam-on and parallel to a wave of that exact size, death is nigh. Fast moving water becomes solid. The ship floats sideways up the sharpening wall; the wall steepens into a precipice topped by an overhanging curl. When caught upside down in that curl of thousands of tons of water, the vessel transforms itself from our violent home on top of the ocean to a silent, wet, black tomb beneath it. Wet death has been the fate of sailors since waterborne craft first went to sea.

This is one way that ships die in a storm: surfing down a steep hill of water into the trough buries the bow ('pearling' in sailing parlance) while a big wave cresting under the stern lifts the fantail high, leaving rudders and screws thrashing fecklessly in the air. The ship, out of balance and no longer steerable, yaws hard and the hull slides parallel into the deep trough beam-on to the wave. The steep curl of the wave, four stories high, rolls the ship upside down like a flipped pancake. The infinite hydraulic power of moving water does not forgive clumsiness in ship handling.

After three of these typhoons, I've learned that they are brutally uncomfortable; one gets exhausted from the eternal tossing, the body constantly working to steady itself, to maintain balance. Sleep is difficult because hanging onto your thin mattress becomes a constant strain. The ship is secured against wind and wave with doors and hatches dogged tight. The air turns stale and hot; fans stir the fetid air to uselessness. Sweat drips from one's head, wetting dungarees—bodies smell. Then somebody across the compartment vomits, which stinks and starts a chain of men vomiting, adding to the misery of a big storm at sea. I've never vomited at sea but I carry a constant headache in rough weather. When I'm not on watch, I take three or four Dramamine tablets and then fall asleep on the steel deck in the privacy of a roaring generator room. My hips are bruised and sore and ache when I awake.

My ship has weathered many storms like this. She is now eighteen years old, with a million sea miles behind her. Her fragile hull is half-inch steel plates riveted together. Built thin, to save weight for a go-fast ship, she is now tired. When steaming at her top speed of thirty-four knots over the surface, she shakes violently, constantly. The hull has rusted in spots, the rust chipped off and repainted many times. Chipping and painting a navy ship is a full-time job; a navy ship is a living organism, and the sea feeds hungrily on steel and aluminum and men's fears. Are there places where the rust has nearly eaten through? Loosened rivets? In its four hundred feet, the ship flexes and bends in the middle. Are there internal ribs, her bones, that have been fatigued and weakened by the continuous flexing caused by the huge waves of a hundred storms like this? Maybe the steel stretches only a ten-thousandth of an inch each time a wave passes. One can watch the expansion joints in the superstructure yawn and close with each big swell. Will this be the storm that breaks her back in two pieces and sinks her? We've lost two destroyers like this one in recent storms. No ship is exempt from sinking in these conditions. Like people, ships weaken and tire in storms. Most days spent in the Pacific are just that—pacific, peaceful. Yet sea states change from glassy smooth to raucous in a few minutes, especially in the Far East. The wind causes waves, and big wind causes big waves. For a sailor, nothing is more frightening than being trapped upside down in total blackness—where up is down and sideways is no ways. Equipment falls, compartments flood, trapped air escapes, the only destiny is drowning in the dark.

We are steaming off Formosa to keep the lid on the contest between Mao's Chinese Communists and Chiang Kai-shek's Nationalists, and maybe to give an edge to Chiang's side. He is now losing.

On the other side of the world, the politicians say we are engaged in a 'Cold War' with the Communists. It is a hot war here along the coast of Red China. The Nationalists and the Communists are shelling each other's islands, Quemoy and Matsu, across the eight miles of coastline that separate them. Intermittently, they blast away with artillery, to little effect except to keep the political pressure on their true believers. East of Formosa, in the South China Sea, our task group of four destroyers works as the anti-submarine and air-defense screen for the aircraft carrier USS Midway. We destroyers are like puppies surrounding their mother; our ship is one-twentieth the size of the capital ship we protect.

Typically, we dog along at twelve knots listening on sonar for enemy submarines. When we hear a sub, we run over the top of it with two destroyers and spook them off or hold them down for a couple of days until they must surface to charge batteries. They are always Russian. When they surface, we photograph their sub and we are always ready to sink them from close range—our guns, anti-submarine rockets, torpedoes, and depth charges are fully armed, our fingers poised above the triggers. As a national policy, we taunt the Russian Bear at every opportunity, daring them to make a wrong move so that our mission can evolve from watching to killing.

When the carrier launches and recovers aircraft, we are assigned to hang a mile behind in her wake while her planes take off and land. If one flames out, or the catapult loses steam, and the plane goes into the water, we send a motor whaleboat to pick up the pilot. Except we have never seen a pilot afloat after a crash. Upon striking the surface, the spinning jet engine inhales water, and the plane unhesitatingly flies beneath the waves. Once we fished out a helmet with the pilot's name on it: "LCDR Martin." A mother somewhere in Indiana cried.

Red Chinese torpedo boats are on the prowl around here and we, with our thin steel skin, are especially vulnerable to these weapons. They scare me. A ton of torpedo is lethal. Underwater, at thirty miles-an-hour, it can come through our tissue-thin skin and bullet into the engine room before exploding.

The unholy anti-submarine alarm screams to the point of pain and knifes into my dense sleep, violently kick-starting my adrenaline pump. I wake and expect to fight a fire at any second even though fighting fire is good news since it means that I didn't die in the initial explosion. While running for my battle station, my hands shake and fumble with the straps of my lifejacket and my heart rattles.

We are a gun platform. There are only four things on this ship: living spaces for men, propulsion equipment, ammunition and fuel oil. We sleep in this powder keg, eat in it, live in it and, in the case of a torpedo strike, die in it. Explosions are devastating—the ship's deck curls back over itself like the top of a sardine can; the men on big ships call us 'tin can sailors' for a reason.

I am a fire control technician, that is, I control the gunfire at targets both above and below the sea's surface. Our surface weapons kill airplanes, ships and land targets. Our underwater weapons kill submarines. I have a battle station at each system. Since we are a relatively small ship our big guns are only five-inchers but we can hit a target accurately ten miles away with a fifty-five-pound projectile. We are primarily a submarine hunter-killer ship, so I also help direct underwater weapons, depth charges and short-distance rockets, against submarines. These deadly toys are exciting as only big and serious weapons of war can be. When we hunt submarines, I am stationed deep in the bowels of the ship surrounded by state-of-the-art computer displays and a hundred electronic amplifiers that process the sonar return signals that show the target's current position and predict the submarine's next actions. Those signals go up to the Combat Information Center where the battle tactics are plotted. My station is the only air-conditioned space on the ship, not for the crew but the computers. It is dim and cool below the water line. We have won best-in-class awards for hunting and killing subs (in exercises of course), but deep down each of us knows that submarines can only be found when they want to be. The killing advantage is all theirs for they can go silent and hide, pulling thermal layers over themselves like a thick blanket. They can wait silently. We can't; our props turn constantly with a unique sound signature. But, after a couple of submerged days, subs run out of battery power to their electric motors and must come up to recharge. Up here on the surface, we can operate for a week without refueling from the oiler that waits on station to rendezvous with the thirsty ships.

Today, in my battle station here at the highest point of the ship's superstructure, four of us are enclosed in the gun director: a rotating turret with a massive telescope that sticks out on both sides and a radar antenna on top. The 'trainer' sits beside me in a tractor seat and rotates the turret left and right. I am the 'pointer' and control the up and down. Both of us spin brass wheels just like you see in the movies. In certain situations I am also the trigger-puller on the big guns. When the gunnery officer barks 'fire,' I squeeze the left trigger twice, which blows a warning horn in the gun turrets and then the right trigger once, which fires the guns. The projectiles leave from inside a ball of fire. They look like hot baseballs that instantly shrink out of sight as they scream away; the ship shudders as if slapped by a giant hand and mirrors below decks shatter from the shock. Beyond the trainer sits the gunnery officer, and behind him is the radar man. At sea, we practice every day so that everything we do becomes routine, automatic, reflexive.

We have spent a lot of time at battle stations out here. Because of the danger that could come our way the guns are loaded, our torpedoes and rockets are armed, our shirt collars are buttoned up tight against flash-fire, and we are ready for combat. Bark the word 'fire' and then stand back to watch our whole floating gun platform belch smoke and flame, airmailing death to the enemy, whoever they might be. My job is to make sure that, ten miles away, my projectiles land within fifty feet of the target and explode, breaking things and killing people.

Today, the director crew, the pointer, trainer, radar man, and gunnery officer are on station in this cramped space. In this storm we can see through our rangefinder, which measures altitude, that the waves are running forty-foot crests. Sometimes a fifty-footer comes along and launches us high, only to plunge us five stories down into the trough beyond.

The weightless drop into the hollow leaves everyone's stomach in the air except for the gunnery officer, Chief Petty Officer Daniel Hoover. His stomach is bulletproof from riding ships for twenty years. A career man, the Chief reminds one of a bulldog; he has a round saggy face, a thick muscular body, and big black unflinching eyes. He is utterly secure in his extensive knowledge of the sea. While his station is gunnery officer, his experience and senior rate at the top of the enlisted men's pyramid gives him power and prestige way above his pay grade. In an environment where many of the officers are college boys, several from Annapolis, he is respected above all of them, except maybe the captain.

Chief Hoover's history adds to his importance. He was stationed on a ship like this one in the largest sea battle in history, the Battle of Leyte Gulf. It was a great fight between the United States and Japan, 367 ships and 1800 planes fought like feral dogs for two days in a hundred thousand square miles of ocean. Ten thousand Japanese and three thousand American sailors died. Just surviving the bloody excitement was heroic. His ship was hit forward by an artillery round, blowing off the bow which became an open mouth, gulping sea water. The ship went pearling at full speed and sank in one minute. As she was being driven under by her own power, the water rising up the superstructure, the chief opened a hatch and casually stepped onto the ocean's surface from the director like the one we are in now. In a short time he was picked up by a destroyer escort and, in the continuing battle, that ship also took a Japanese round through the stern that exploded a powder magazine, and he found himself once again ejected into the sea. Maybe five people survived out of two hundred.

He was picked up by a third ship. After being pulled aboard, he crawled into a 40mm gun tub and began passing ammunition to the loaders.

He is one of the few people who make me feel that being a destroyer sailor is okay. He is close to a minor god for me; my respect for him is infinite. I once asked him if he was scared in Leyte Gulf. He leveled his dark eyes, his brow fell, and in a gravelly monotone he answered, "Is the Pope Catholic?" I never asked him again. So it is with real survivors. They don't talk much. Sometimes never.

When the ship rolls beyond forty-five degrees, the hair on the sailor's neck instinctively begins to tingle. In this storm, the motion of the superstructure is magnificent in its magnitude, the three axis of motion—pitch, roll, and yaw—magnified by the height of our station above the sea. We swing in eighty-foot arcs. Encapsulated by steel machinery, we bruise our shoulders and elbows as we bang around inside the tight quarters, getting punched by sharp corners.

The pitching, rolling and yawing gets worse. My stomach is in rebellion, loading up nausea's big gun. I don't think it will stay down much longer. I've been seasick a lot but only with headaches. I've never gotten used to the ocean's restlessness but I've also never tossed my cookies. In the mess hall, as the pork chops floating in grease slide back and forth in their tin trays, I have been arrogant, chiding my shipmates about their weak stomachs. They green up and escape from the sickening smells of the mess deck to run topside where they hang over the lifelines and return everything except their souls to the angry ocean.

An unusually big wave hits the bow at an angle. We lift buoyantly, almost triumphantly, and then slide sideways down the cliff-face of the wave. The vessel slews into the trough. We roll hard and keep rolling further. I know we must be at forty degrees, but we keep listing harder...forty-two degrees...forty-four degrees...I stretch my hand out to the bulkhead to stay in my seat. I glance over at my trainer. His mouth is slack, his eyes wide in terror...forty-five degrees...forty-six degrees...she can now lose the battle to save herself. The further she rolls the less she wants to come back upright. Will she come back? Or will she violently roll upside down? She hesitates there for a long moment...a hesitating moment that seems like minutes...maybe forever. At this angle, she's going to turn turtle. I can feel it. I hear the trainer mumble under his breath, a whiny, "Ohgod...ohgod...ohgod..."

In reflex, I check the top buckle of my life vest.

And then it's over. As we top the wave crest the righting moment kicks in and the little ship slowly fights back into balance. I realize that I have had my hand on the hatch lever, automatically thinking about going through it, stepping off the turret onto the ocean's surface just like the chief did in Leyte.

I snap a look at Chief Hoover's unchangeable face. He looks bored.

"Chief, I'm very sorry, but I have to toss," I say. "I don't have a choice."

I feel around and find the coffee can the crew keeps stashed up here for just such notable occasions. I pull it close to me and peer into its shiny interior.

This typhoon is beating me. I am embarrassed to be so weak, so soft and yielding to its attacks. And in front of an American hero.

"Go ahead," he says looking straight ahead, "It's happened to all of us."

6 for 5

The navy always pays its sailors in cash. I stand at the end of the pay-line and, as each man comes by, I tell him what he owes. Once he counts out his debt and hands it to me, I mark him *'paid in full, 9-15-57'* in my loan book. 'Thank yous' are nonexistent. Sometimes the borrowers look away from me since I am the person who financed their transgressions. Thanklessness is just part of the business; the business of borrowing to pay for prostitutes who satisfy the men who are married to women with kids, back home. The loan business is like that; you can't tell people how to spend their money.

The four destroyers in my division rotate from Pearl Harbor, in and out of the western Pacific every four months, to the oceans around Japan, Australia, Philippines and some islands with forgettable names. We are getting deeper into a cold war and the nuclear race with the Russians, and it looks like the world could burn up before the Fifties are over.

Japan is about sex. In Sasebo, Yokosuka and other port towns, prostitution is socially acceptable, or at least tolerated by the locals. A sailor's money is way too good for anyone to climb onto one's moral high horse—that horse has no riders in Japanese culture. And regarding the local economy, two businesses are guaranteed to bring in regular income: bars and prostitution.

For the sailor, both of these require 'walking around' money. Often, when appetite remains at the end of the money, a loan can be arranged for a week or two from a shipmate less lusty and a bit more conservative.

Sitting on the highest point on the ship, I watch the comings and goings of sailors living the sailors' life: leaving on liberty rambunctious and laughing; returning from the beach broke, hungover, and depressed. Then, their thirst for booze and women unslaked, borrowing money from whomever they can to return to the beach and further indulge their appetites. The customary arrangement is $5 loaned today in return for $7 repayment on payday, which is usually a week or less away.

I do not know how to calculate interest, but this seemed a lot to pay for such a short time. Because I'm not a pussy-hound, I've spent my time touring the cities and making touristy photos to sell to my shipmates, so I have a few bucks to spare. One day, awhile back, walking a narrow street in Yokosuka, I ran into a shipmate who hit me for a $10 loan.

"So, I owe you $14 on payday?" he asked.

I knew he was married and sent most of his money home each payday.

"No, that's too much..." I said, "...just give me $12. That's enough."

And that's how it started. Word travelled around the crew and thereafter men would borrow from me at the reduced rate of 6 for 5. They were happy. I was happy. The bartenders and mama-sans were happy. The officers were unhappy until I started loaning money to them because loaning money at interest was against navy regulations—they, too, were at the mercy of their maleness.

A hundred members of our ship's crew are married; they are accustomed, more or less, to having regular sex with their wives and here, relief so anonymously available with the young Japanese girls, they see no need to change that part of their lives.

Marriage is a half a world away and the married men, like the rest of us, are at the mercy of their genes and their defined role in human existence.

Whorehouses and their inhabitants exist world-wide. In some countries, they operate inside compounds. The pretty ones work inside, the old ugly ones work the streets. In Japan, they usually operate downtown in traditional wooden houses of cedar and tile roofs. Inside, the houses are pure Zen: perfectly proportioned, functional without decoration. Sliding rice-paper partitions, and polished wood floors covered with tatami mats, give the impression of a design philosophy seasoned by fifty centuries of civilization. An altar in the corner, elegantly spare, bears an incense stick standing vertical in a bowl, a single flower bending in a vase, or a framed, stilted photograph, fading to gray, of a grandfather in a combat cap or a child in a sailor suit.

The girls, usually young and olive skinned, seem to be farmers' daughters making their way in the city. Most of them are not especially pretty, but passable; their best makeup is early evening's half-light. They laugh and giggle at everything, fire your cigarettes, refill your beer glass, and place their hand on you to show the other girls that you are claimed for the hour or the evening.

They live in the house and go to work when there are guests. Mama-san collects all monies, herself an ex-hooker, and occasionally, when an older sailor wants to sample her decades of expertise, he buys her services for triple the going rate of a young woman. The mama-san is God and rules like one. Mercilessly kidded by the customers, she laughs good-naturedly, flashes gold teeth, collects money, pours drinks and keeps the swabbies calm. It is all very pleasant, like a family gathering in an Iowa living room.

Fights among the men are rare since their libidos have already been assuaged or will be soon, so there is nothing to be contentious about. If alcohol makes a sailor too rowdy for the mama-san, there is always a little Japanese guy in baggy clothes who comes out of a back room to use you for judo practice.

The customers at this house are all enlisted men, boys, really, just out of high school. Some of them simply sit and talk, some play cards, some drink beers, catch a 'short time' and leave. Officers have their own house.

It is surprisingly easy to fall in love with women who do not act like American women. Japanese women respond culturally in ways that women at home do not. These Buddhists are emotionally self-contained, they exist in the Zen and require almost no emotional tending. They live for their men, even during temporary liaisons, and enjoy being servants to the pairing. They answer every request for sex and perform skillfully without delay.

When one hires their services, the customers are coddled, entertained, protected and physically satisfied. It is not surprising that a sailor will borrow money to indulge this nirvana. He will have another payday in a week or two and much of that time will be spent at sea so why the hell not?

Back home, while heavy necking and petting are normal, real penetration—sex before marriage—is a very big and dangerous undertaking. The price of pregnancy in the 50's is prohibitive: marriage or death from the barrel of Daddy's shotgun and, or, lifetime support for an unwanted child. Condoms wrapped in endless hope are carried in billfolds until they rot and only the ring remains.

All of us wished there was some way to have sex without the egregious price to be paid for it. Japan had the answer. Easy, guiltless, available sex.

For 180 yen, about five bucks, Peanuts is very solicitous. She has a big toothy smile and boney legs from years of malnutrition and the customary habit of squatting on her haunches, which cuts off the circulation below her knees.

Inside her rice paper cubicle, she bends over and rolls out a futon on top of the tatami. In the half-light, her malnourished bottom shows the sustained hunger of her farm life.

"You like me?" she asks.

"Yes," I say. "You are very pretty."

"You like screw?"

Pulling her blouse over her head, she removes her shapely western breasts and hangs them on a wall hook.

"Yes."

"How you like screw?"

She stands close and touches my groin. Like all Japanese on a fish and seaweed diet, her breath and body have the smell of a tidal plain.

"You like shakuhachi?"

"I don't know…" I am new to this sport. "…Just regular, I guess."

"I do you," she says. And she does. Her ministrations are expert, cursory and quick. And so am I.

In my bunk aboard ship, I think back on Peanuts. She was a really cute girl, very happy. She liked me. I like her more now than I did when we were together. I would like to get to know her. To talk with her, to hold her hand and walk down the street, to have her show me the sights and translate the day into simple fun. I decide to go back to the house and find Peanuts, buy her out of the house for the day, pay Mama-san for her escape.

At the door, I say, "Mama-san, I want to visit Peanuts."

She shakes her head, "No Peanuts here," she says sadly.

"She was here just yesterday afternoon," I say. "I saw her. I visited her."

"No. Peanuts not here. Peanuts gone."

"Where did she go?"

Mama-san shrugs and shakes her head, "Peanuts no live here. Peanuts go to home. Mama sick," and she turns away.

Just my luck, I think.

Subic Bay, Philippines was about San Miguel Beer and VD. After watching the infected men line up at morning sick call to get their shots, I didn't even go ashore. When you went to sick bay for treatment, you were on medical restriction and couldn't get liberty, so your playtime was over for ten days.

I avoided that place like the plague it distributed.

On the other hand, Sydney was about beauty and love and a major blessing for American sailors. At the time I knew that it would leave a scar on my brain, I just didn't know what kind.

The Battle of the Coral Sea was a turning point for the Aussies in the Pacific War. The Japanese were cruising down to Port Moresby, New Guinea, just north of Australia, to seize control of that part of the world and seemed to have it in the bag when the Japanese warships were intercepted by the American fleet immediately west of Australia in the Coral Sea. In that hot battle, we lost ships and planes and so did the invaders but the Japanese fleet had to save itself and turn away from the Aussie and American guns, saving Australia from invasion by the Yellow Peril. It was a very close thing. The Aussies hate the Japanese.

Coral Sea Day is a remembrance of that fight. And our ships are invited into Sydney Harbor to help celebrate this important fifteenth anniversary of Australian Salvation.

As our four warships ease up to the concrete dock in downtown Sydney, we can see that inside a fenced security area there are a thousand women waving a smiling welcome to us. We have never seen anything like this. We look at each other and raise our eyebrows in approval and grin. There are innumerable possibilities of love suggested by those many smiling female faces. A close look into the crowd reveals that every beautiful woman in Queensland is here. And they ain't here for autographs; they are here for us.

Shay is twenty-two, a gorgeous photographer's model, simply stunning. In a King's Cross lounge we hit it right off, liking each other immediately. After a few drinks, we migrate to a bench in the park overlooking Bondi Beach. We kiss tenderly, I hold her close and carefully and gently feel her lovely breasts. After an evening of closeness and connection, she wants to show me where she lives so the next afternoon we taxi to her home in Manley Beach.

Her modest house is white, and sparkly clean just like her mother. The smallish woman greets me with a cordial smile and suspicious eyes.

As I shake the mother's hand, Shay says, "Mum, this is Jerry. We're getting married!"

Mum doesn't change her expression, only tilts her head: "Would you like a cuppa?"

"Yes ma'am, that would be nice."

Get married? I'm a sailor! In three more days, I'm going back to sea. While I would like to make love to this gorgeous animal, getting married is not in the picture. It becomes an awkward afternoon but I can't keep my eyes off her. It is exciting just looking at her, watching her body move inside her diaphanous dress.

When I return to the ship, I find women everywhere in various stages of undress who are not supposed to be aboard this military vessel loaded with explosives. There are women topside and below, on the bridge, on the weather decks, in the sonar and radar spaces, in the gun turrets, the fantail, and the crews quarters. It is sexual heaven. The ship is now Fletcher Christian's 1788 sailing ship Bounty overrun by the naked women of Tahiti. The Aussie women make it clear they would be like to be taken to America and live in the land of promise. In uniform we all look the same and in the hopes of love, aggressive female flesh yields to country boys from the deep South who have nothing back home except an old car. Competition between the women is polite but insistent. They are fighting against the shortness of time and thinking, "We have to fall in love fast, before the ship leaves. We must use every feminine wile to create instant love."

I step below to my bunk in the crew's quarters and, through the forest of bunks hanging on chains, I hear rhythmic squeaking and a woman's sing-song voice: "Alabama…I love saying it…Alabama…Alabama…I love hearing it…Alabama."

Their plan works. After five days in Sydney, of 235 officers and men, a hundred of them already married, 190 engagements have been agreed to. Once we are back at sea, tough, grown men lie in their bunks and weep, crying real tears of loss for their

Aussie loves, the same eyes that were completely dry when they were leaving their wives standing on the dock in Hawaii.

Shay and I write a few times but what can a man say when he knows he will never see a woman again. "I will return, I promise."

She sends me pictures signed in a studied high-school script, 'Love Always, Shay.' One in particular stands out: she is leaning fetchingly back against a dock piling, her leg bent, wearing a white bathing suit, her dark hair falling across her naked shoulders, the smiling picture of a perfect bathing beauty. On the back: "*Manly Beach, 1957. Love you forever,* XOXOXOXO"

My loan business is booming. The magic combination for sailors is Australian women and borrowed money. I loan $4000 out every two weeks which makes me four to five hundred a week. My navy pay is $155 a month. I am running the largest slush fund in the Pacific Fleet and am awash in cash. My locker is stuffed with it. At the end of the pay line, I collect so much cash I have to unbutton my shirt and stuff the cash inside until I look lumpy and pregnant.

Conflicts with borrowers are very rare. Many times I forgive debts to keep the peace. Most of my customers are honest and they honor their debts. Occasionally there is a bad debtor but I don't worry about them much since, through good loans and bad, we still have to live with each other, to work together, our elbows touching in hot radar spaces. On a sinking ship, unlike land combat, everyone swims together in burning oil, officers and enlisted men, tall and short, black and white, borrowers and lenders, believers and atheists.

Upon seeing my withholding tax statement, which shows my navy income for the year, I realize I have spent more money on high-end camera equipment than my annual navy income and that my very profitable business was making me more money than the captain, which was bound to anger the ship's officers.

At one point, I look up at the bridge and see the captain watching me collect money. It gives me a bad feeling. Navy life has a different morality from civilian life. The rules are: 'it's not what you do; it's what you get caught doing.' One day the master-at-arms, the ship's senior cop, pulls me aside and whispers, "Navy Intelligence just came aboard. It's a Lieutenant JG who just got assigned into the gunnery department but the duty yeoman says actually he's undercover from the flagship. He's here to bust you."

This is serious news. Very serious.

How do I handle this? My most deeply indebted people were probably the most likely to talk. I immediately go to each of them and say, "Flag has sent NI to arrest me. But they can't make a case without witnesses. Keep your mouth shut and I'll call us even. Okay?"

"Okay."

After a week the lieutenant leaves empty-handed. It cost me a few hundred but I'm still in business.

Our division of four destroyers rotate in and out of Pearl Harbor, we stay there eight months at a stretch and then move on to WesPac for four. Waikiki Beach is eight miles from our dock and if a man owns a car, life can be pretty good: drive into Honolulu, stash your uniform in a locker, don a disgustingly loud Hawaiian shirt printed with weird flowers and you're ready for action.

Enlisted men can't bring cars onto the base so they park them on the street outside the gate. When their ships are deployed, the sailor's cars have to be moved or they will be impounded or towed away. Thus, I decide that the used car business could be a good one. I can buy and sell for cash and I have a continuous supply and steady market. Galloping collateral is unheard of. This is an island. Where are they going to go? Besides, most of the sailors' cars are only a step above junk.

The buy side is simple: There are always sailors trying to sell their vehicles for the two hundred to five hundred dollars they have in them. The longer they wait, the more likely their ship will sail and the car will be gone forever. So the asking prices drop dramatically in the week before sailing. I simply walk aboard their ship and ask, "Who has a car to sell?"

There are always sellers. Some easy negotiation ensues but usually we settle on half of what the seller paid for the car; I pay him in cash and collect his signed title with the buyer's name left open. The next week, I walk over to the ships newly arrived from WesPac and ask who would like to buy a car? There are always plenty of men who dream about the beach and women and freedom. I charge whatever the market value is, usually twice what I paid. I fill in the buyer's name on the title certificate and hand it to the new owner.

Can't pay for the whole thing? That's okay. Just make a good down payment, I'll loan you the balance for a month or two at 6 for 5.

My second trip to Australia was different. A Brisbane newspaperman came aboard to interview sailors and he commanded me in no uncertain terms: "Go to Surfer's Paradise, you won't believe the women there." I flew.

There were rooms full of bored women listening to dumb little jazz bands in that seaside resort. When we sailors walked in, every female eye turned to appraise us. In return for our appraisal of their smiling faces they opened their legs to show their panties, even occasionally flashing an inviting dark patch. These women know their market. While we Americans know little about Australian culture, they know that Americans are at mercy of our Puritan culture, where sex is holy and hard to come by. Here they make it easy and joyful. Heaven. Back on the ship we quietly admit to each other, "When I get out, I'm coming back here to live."

I didn't fall in love or receive a marriage proposal or meet a girl's mother, instead I got picked out by a divorced night-club singer ten years my senior.

She wore a long dress with a long slit that flashed a sexy leg and I stayed up through the night to catch her act. During our intimate moments in the wee hours, she screamed so loudly in her singer's voice that her neighbors thought she was being tortured. She called herself the Blonde Canary. So did I.

We promised we would meet again in Tokyo where she had a gig the next month. You know how sailors lie. She sent a sexy photograph signed with her stage name. That meeting never happened.

I'm lying in my bunk when I feel a hand on my shoulder. It's Hammerslagen.

"What?" I growl.

"I need to borrow some money."

"Forget it, Hammer. You already owe me a bunch of money and you haven't paid up in months. Get away from me."

"No, you have to loan me twenty bucks."

"Why?"

"Because I feel hot."

"Wadda you mean, hot?"

"There is a crap game going on in after-steering and I feel hot. I can win today. I know it. I feel it."

"Bullshit. Catch up what you owe and we'll talk about it."

"How much do I owe?"

"The last time I looked you owed me two-hundred-sixty dollars. Repay that and we'll talk about some more."

"How did it get to be that much?"

"Because, Hammer, when you don't pay every payday, the interest adds onto the whole amount. I told you that at the beginning."

He begins to look desperate, shifting his weight from one foot to the other.

"Please loan me some money. I have to get into this game. I know these guys. They're losers. I've beat 'em before. And I'm hot, I can feel it. I can't lose. Please, please give it to me."

A tear appears in his eye. Is it real?

"Goddam, Hammer, I hate to see a grown man beg. Here's the twenty. Don't ever ask me for money again. This is it. Just stay away from me."

"Oh, Jesus. Thank you." He disappears into where the crap game is rolling on a wool blanket, surrounded by crouching sailors blowing on the dice and cajoling the cubes to tumble right.

I fall asleep but am shaken awake by a hand on my shoulder. I crack my eyes.

"I thought I told you to stay away from me, Hammerschlagen. Wadda you want now? I ain't givin' you any more goddam money."

"I don't need more. I beat the shit outta the snipes from the black gang and won all your money back. Here's your two hundred and eighty bucks." He places a stack of bills on my chest. "Mark me paid in your little asshole book."

My last year in the service, when I wasn't standing duty aboard, I worked nights as a darkroom monkey for a fine photographer with a studio in the Hawaiian Village Hotel owned by Henry Kaiser. I learned to develop and print and be critical of photographs, to tell the difference between good and bad. I watched movie stars come and go, met politicians, actors, Elvis and Henry Kaiser. And I loved it. In a meeting with Mr. Kaiser, he told me he had started his working career as a photographer. Teenagers went crazy over Elvis, stalking him like feral animals; Liz Taylor and Mike Todd preened and posed just as stars are supposed to do in public.

A few months before my enlistment was up, I rented an apartment across the park from the photo studio on Waikiki Beach. Rather than take my official separation from the Navy back in Treasure Island and then return to Colorado on the government dime, I saw no reason to go back home when I lived in a little slice of heaven: on the beach with a job learning my chosen profession of photography and the girl with the nice body across the courtyard who would drop by for sex.

The ship's yeoman issued my orders and I stepped from the ship onto the dock in Pearl Harbor a free man after four years and thirty minutes of duty and regimentation.

I drove home to my rented apartment on Waikiki Beach, walked into the kitchen, stripped my dress blues to the middle of the kitchen floor, swept them out the back door and slipped on beach shorts, my favorite attire.

CLUB MED

Governor's Harbor, a watery indent into the coast of Eleuthera, is a quiet place in quiet water with many anchored sailboats and yachts populated by spoiled rich people. Across the bay, Club Med rests white and low along the sand. Today, six vacationing French tourists from over there, in search of laughs, booze, and sex, buzz around the harbor astride a huge air-inflated weenie, sun-reddened and screaming with the thrill of being towed at high speed by a powerful motorboat. They weave in and out of the anchored sailboats making waves that tip wineglasses and piss everyone off in what, without them, would be a nearly idyllic, peaceful refuge.

Disgusted by this unnecessary disturbance, as they roar closely by and rock my boat for the fourth time, I stand on the bow, hang onto to the forestay, drop my filthy shorts to my ankles and, holding it in my hand, I waggle my manhood at them.

As they speed by I yell, "You fuckin' Frogs!"

The women's eyes fly wide open, and their mouths drop.

I get laughs and thumbs-up from the boat crews anchored nearby. The Frogs don't come back to this part of the bay.

It has been a hard passage to here. I'm beaten up badly. I haven't eaten in a day or so. I can't remember. My attitude is thin; my outlook black; I'm neutral to living, dying, danger, love, hate, even heartbreak. I need to get drunk and forget the darkness in my head. The Gulf Stream was more harrowing than I ever imagined it could be. My boat at the mercy of the surf break of West End, and my life sliding toward the rocks on the shore, these images haunt my sleep. And anchor paranoia floats in the back of my mind like ground fog. The fear of an anchor slipping, allowing my boat to go adrift in the dark while I'm asleep, has been keeping me in a fitful state of half-wakefulness. Every hour, I get up, turn a sextant on its side and measure the angle between this near light on the beach and that other light further down, and read the difference in degrees of arc. A couple of hours later I get up and take another reading to see if the first and second readings match, assuming that if the anchor slips the angle between the lights will change. Even when the first and second readings match exactly I don't believe them. I check and recheck. The doubt grows bigger each time. Anchor paranoia owns my mind. Big fish hunt at night and are keenly attracted to lights; it is a really dangerous time to have to go down and check. I'm nervous. At midnight, I don a snorkel and mask, dive into the fifteen feet of water and, with a flashlight, pull myself down the anchor line to shine the light and check that the anchor is still securely buried and isn't walking out of the bottom like it did up in Long Cay.

On that quiet evening, a glorious sunset scattering gold around me, I'd anchored in twenty feet of water using two Danforth anchors, one anchor set out to port, another set opposite to starboard, both cleated to the bow by sixty-foot lines. In the dead of that night, the wind shifted around to onshore and built dramatically to twenty knots. In the wind my little boat bucked and yawed back and forth on the anchor lines, by turns tightening one and slacking the other, the waves breaking noisily along the hull. Meantime I slept with a naïve confidence—I had anchored well and felt certain the boat couldn't move.

A sharp bang brought me awake into a bright morning. I ran topside and, looking back over the stern, saw that my rudder was buried in sand. The boat was aground. The weeds were under my fantail, my boat inching further and further onto the dry sand with each pounding wave.

Looking forward, my anchor lines were no longer opposite each other at 9 and 3 o'clock, they stretched away together from the bow, now parallel at twelve. As the boat hunted back and forth in the wind, the anchors had walked through the sand, first one then the other, eventually coming parallel during the night. I had started at least fifty yards from the beach in fifteen feet of water; now there were three feet between us and the bottom and waves were splashing up on the beach under my stern.

Now, I see danger everywhere. A beer is what I need.

My life raft is a one-man plastic blowup kayak, an off-brand named SeaEagle. (I have a buddy named Sam Siegle. Thus, I name this rubber kayak my Jewcanoe after him.)

I paddle over to the beach in my kayak and walk into a dark and primitive bar. It is empty except for a younger man at a back table who nurses a bottle. I join him.

"Hey, whot's happinin'?"

"Everthin' and nothin'," he says in an Aussie accent, almost under his breath. He looks worn. I know I look drawn and ratty, too. My hair hasn't been cut in weeks and hangs slick and greasy as do my shorts. Even my friends wouldn't recognize me in this shape.

The conversation goes easily.

I ask, "You sailin'?"

"Yes."

"Single-handing?"

He nods.

"What size boat are you sailin'?"

"A twenty-one."

Wow, I think, his boat is even smaller than mine.

"Where'd ya come in from?"

"Sidney."

"Sidney where?"

"Australia."

"Where?"

He looks hard at me. "Australia," he says sharply, "Down under, mate. Ever heard of it?"

I look carefully at his face to see if he is kidding me. He isn't. His face is a tan noncommittal mask.

"Jesus, you are shittin' me! You sailed a little boat from Australia to here by yourself? Christ, man, that's halfway around the world!"

He nods agreement and looks at his beer bottle.

"What possessed you to use such a small boat? Why in God's name did you do this?" I asked.

"I wanted to. I am a brickie and I got bored. This was the boat I owned," he said.

He looks out at the masts rocking on the crystalline water. "I wanted to sail around the world," he says absently.

Around the world. I can't imagine doing that.

"Has that been scary?"

He shrugged, "Yes, it 'uz dodgy sometimes, mate."

"Were you scared that you'd die out there?"

He took on a distant look, "It's part of the adventure, mate, and dyin' is just one factor in life, you know. If a man is good enough he can outthink death. Take away death and it isn't an adventure anymore." He tips his head back and pulls long on the beer. "I don't have anything to go home to." His eyes go blank, "I may never go back."

I stare into him, searching for some wisdom accumulated from sailing half way around the world in a tiny boat, some eternal truth, some insight into the meaning of life. His eyes are two doors into a vacant room, a void without feeling, a negative space, an emotional desert. All Aussies are nuts I think.

At that moment, I realize all single-handers are nuts; really, they have to be insane. Single handers float alone in a universe of their own creation. But I'm not crazy like him. While I feel empty, deep down I know that I am still susceptible to stark, paralyzing fear although it is getting harder for fear to win the battle against logic. Is that a dangerous thing? I don't know.

I drain my beer and wave, "I'll see ya' around…good luck."

Back in my berth, I listen to the gentle lap of the small waves and the incessant ding…ding…ding of the halyard slapping against the mast. Other than the crazy bastard in the bar, I haven't spoken to another human being in days. I am truly alone even with all these boats around. Nobody here knows my name. The awareness of how easy it is to die unconnected in an uncaring ocean is dissolving into a craving for company, the company of regular people who don't sail.

Club Med is right over there, within walking distance. Maybe I'll see the Frogs. Over there is a real world with drinks and women and music and women.

I clean up as best I can, take a bath in Joy dish detergent, dig out my wrinkled suntan pants and collared shirt, comb my hair. Then I paddle to the beach and walk around the bay to the fancy entrance and pay the gate guard the ten-dollar visitor's fee; he places a string of colored beads around my neck, a substitute for money at this club.

Inside, the music is loud with a tropical beat. I work my way to the bar through writhing dancing bodies bouncing to the conga drums.

From the corner of the bar, I watch the dancers; actually, I watch the women. They are only partially clothed, their breasts bouncing, legs flashing above bare feet, made-up faces flushed and smiling. Certainly, one of them will walk up and ask me to dance when she recognizes that I am a real sailor, not a wannabe from the city. That will be the beginning of a wonderfully sexy night. Boy, am I ready for some girl action.

Two stools away, the only other people at the bar are a small man speaking with a shapely young woman. Their faces are close, and there is an aura of impending intimacy about them.

Facing the man, the small woman laughs, throws her head back and talks quickly, gesticulating excitedly. The back of her hand slaps her drink and it splashes across the bar, drowning her money beads.

Embarrassed, she exclaims, "Oh, my...I'm sooo sorry."

The man pats her hand, "Not to worry; we'll get another."

The French barkeep rags the bar, soaks up the icy detritus, and in a new glass, mixes her a fresh tropical drink and sets it on the bar. He then snaps off some of her colored pay beads.

I motion the bartender close so he can hear me over the drums. "In polite bars, when a woman accidentally spills her drink, the house gladly sets her up a new one without charge," I say.

He tosses a smile, "I saw her do that on purpose," he says.

"That's bullshit. I saw her do it. She didn't mean to do it. It was an accident."

He gives me a hard look, "Yes she did. She did it on purpose," he says coldly.

There are times when action, however unpleasant, is required by the circumstances of the moment. Many times while sailing I've have been compelled to do things that had to be done. I had no choice if life was to go on as before.

With a forefinger, I signal the barman to bend closer to me. When his face is close to mine, I reach over, bunch his collar in my fist, pull him sliding across the top of the bar and drop him to the floor. He hits the deck with a grunt. It is all rather workmanlike. I'm not angry. Like checking the anchor set, this is simply a chore that has to be done.

With my knee in his chest, I cock my right fist to feed this man a knuckle sandwich. I am seized by muscular hands; men in uniform are on me, pinning my arms, a foot in my back, my face rubbing the floor.

In the hammerlock of the guards, they frog march me back to the gate. I expand my chest and shoulders to try to be bigger and meaner.

"That fuckin' Frog needed to get his ass whipped," I say to them.

Outside the gate, they release my arms. "Don't come back…" the bigger of the two huge black men orders as he shoves me out the gate and onto the sandy road.

My shoulder is tweaked from the action. Walking back to the boat, I try to shake it out. But I feel refreshed, even renewed, well ready to compete against the vagaries of big wind and waves that occasionally try to kill me. It is the first time on this trip that I have felt fully confident. Even arrogant.

I shoulda hit that Frog, I think. Give him an Old Man's uppercut like I was taught or a flashing left hook; that wiseass would've never seen it coming; his first hint would have been blood running from a cut cheek. With any luck it would have left a scar; something to remember me by; a lesson to be polite to small women and small men like me.

DENVER START

As the hired photographer (and acrophobic), the higher I climb on the hundred-foot derrick, the slicker underfoot it becomes; grease thrown from the spinning steel wheels and cables coats everything including the exposed, outside ladder to the top. My shoes slip sideways on the ladder rungs, my hands lose their grip, and my fingers nearly release and drop me to the drilling floor ten stories below. Finally standing on the top of this drilling rig and its spinning crown block, the rig trembles nervously as the full weight of eight thousand feet of drill stem, some 160,000 pounds, plunges deep into the borehole and the total weight hangs on the derrick; I can feel the heavy stress on this quivering giant through my feet.

The view from up here is a featureless plane of sagebrush meeting a threatening dark sky along a ruler-straight desert horizon. The raincloud above this drilling site threatens to send lightning down to the rig; if that happens, it will come right through me.

Since leaving Art Center School, in Hollywood, I've considered myself to be an advertising photographer until this very moment, when I realize that I am a complete fool, a living lightning rod; no photograph is worth being lit up like a fluorescent tube and fried by electricity but I am desperate because I finally have an assignment that pays real money.

I began this adventure with these simple words: "Mr. Art Director, give me jobs that other photographers have screwed up, that didn't fulfill the assignment, that didn't work, that didn't please you. If my photo-illustrations do not work for you, there is no charge," I say.

Each summer morning I dress in the only suit I own: a heavy tweed number, $37 from JC Penny, a home-ironed shirt and a cheap tie. I place a black telephone in the middle of the kitchen table alongside the Yellow Pages opened to 'advertising agencies.' My hand rests on the phone, and I wait for 9AM. My objective is to call and make appointments with every art director, or any conceivable photography buyer, no matter how remote the possibility, to present my school portfolio. I show ten pieces of school work; none applicable to real advertising use I later learn.

I'm as ignorant of national economics as I am of advertising but soon learn that we're in the middle of the 1962 recession. I cannot give away a photograph with a $5 bill clipped to it. Potential buyers ask my price: it's the going Denver market rate for photography assignments: $100 a day plus expenses for props and models at cost. They politely take my business card and then, I am sure, file it in the trash can. After presenting my work two dozen times in the first month, I haven't sold one assignment. Even if I am the worst salesman in the city I should be able to sell something. Is there something wrong with me?

Bad news. I have gout in both hips from eating pinto beans for a year and I walk in constant pain. I also have a wife and a baby boy. We live in a $75 a month basement apartment with newly varnished floors that reflect like bowling lanes. A kitchen table, two chairs and two borrowed canvas camp cots, lent by the landlord, are the only furniture. Tiny Taz sleeps on a folded blanket in a cardboard box on the floor.

I have no choice but to succeed and I have no idea how to do that.

To be a photographer I have to shoot. To shoot, it appears that I have to gamble. Starvation is imminent and I am forced to rethink my selling proposition so I develop the sales plan of "Just try me…try me for free."

Some art directors laugh at me, and each of them, in one way or another, says "Man, with that idea you will quickly go broke in this town."

There is no money. I'm already a failure. Because I don't know what else to do I just keep doing, calling people, talking, hunting down and pitching anyone who might buy photography.

Calling on an art director I had called on two or three times before, this time, he looks up from his drawing board and says, "Oooookay. My client is a cryogenic firm and they sell this supercooled stuff. I need a photo of cryogenic bubbles boiling up into the air from a beaker of liquid nitrogen. Other photographers have tried and failed. Crap…they gave us unusable crap. You can try it if you want. If you decide to try, we'll need this illustration by Monday." He taps his layout; his gaze is challenging, "But you know you are going to die doing this, don't you? In this town, with your little creative proposition, they'll steal you blind."

I look him in the eye: "I hear you. But you aren't going to steal, and that's the only thing that matters…see you on Monday."

As I walk out the door he says, "Just remember, if it doesn't work for me you are doing it for nothing!" I turn and give him a thumb's up.

The photography problem he gives me is this: a layout artist with color pencils can quickly illustrate gas bubbling off a liquid, expanding into visible gas bubbles above the surface, getting bigger in the open air.

In real life, however, no such thing occurs. The bubbles expand as they ascend to the surface of the liquid, pop, and pass into the atmosphere as a transparent gas. There ain't no bubbles growing in the air. Ever.

Over a weekend I try several experiments to see if I can produce the effect the art director has drawn: the bubbles expanding in the air as rendered in his imagination. Nothing I try works. There was nothing that will or can produce that image.

Dejected, I drink a beer at the bar around the corner and watch the amber bubbles form and rise in the glass. They start small and expand as they ascend and end up in a layer of foam. An idea takes hold.

At the pet store, I buy a small square fish tank. At the liquor store, I buy a six-pack. At the studio, I fill the fish tank with beer and photograph the backlighted bubbles that form on the glass and then rise. When I print the illustration, I mount it upside down so that the big bubbles from the bottom of the tank show at the top. On Monday, I deliver the complex assignment. The director is surprised and delighted and hands me another shooting layout, the oil rig

There are no huzzahs for me resulting from this brilliant start in my advertising career. I needed the money too badly; it was all about sheer relief.

Later, on one of my presentation patrols, I walk uninvited into an old house in an aging neighborhood off Eighth Avenue with a small ad agency sign on the door. I ask to speak to the art director. The receptionist points at the ceiling. "On the second floor. A tall man in sunglasses, he's the studio owner," she says without looking up from her typewriter.

I launch into my pitch, he listens and nods occasionally. Leaning back in his squeaky office chair and flipping through my ten show prints, he asks, "How's it goin' for ya?"

"Actually, not very well," I say. "I'm not getting hired. I keep tryin', but it isn't working. I know there is work out there. I see the ads hanging on their display walls but I ain't gettin' none of it."

He nods, "The Denver market is hurting in this recession. Everybody's tight,"

He looks out the attic window. "How much are you charging?"

"The standard rates here in the city, a hundred a day plus props and models. But, my proposition is that my photos must work for your purpose, or the shoot is free. I guarantee all of my illustrations to work as you require. And, you get full rights. You own the photos outright, the negatives, transparencies everything. I don't charge use fees. No cure, no pay!"

He looked at me for a long time from inside the dark glasses, then laughed. "Well, that may be the going rate but it isn't enough. Here's the problem you have…," looking at the ceiling and shaking his head, he takes me to school. "There is no reason for any art director to use you. Agencies make money by marking up your invoice which makes them a minimum of a fifteen percent service fee for hiring you. They would rather mark up a big invoice than a small one." With pale eyes, he looks at me over his dark glasses, "Got it?"

"Got it."

"Where's your studio located?"

"I don't have a studio; I can only shoot on location." He nods.

"We have an empty basement here. I'll rent it to you for fifty a month."

I look at him for a long time. Finally, I say, "I don't have fifty dollars."

"That's okay. We can trade out the rent."

In that half-hour, I was transformed from a photographer working out of the trunk of his car to a downtown studio photographer. I was delirious. Until I saw the bird carcass.

The old cellar smelled just like any old basement, musty, dusty, with an edge of acrid in the air. It had not been cleaned in years. Feathers of a woodpecker that had pecked his last wood years ago were scattered everywhere, in the air, on the floor, and in the joist bridging overhead. The low ceiling would be a serious limitation. The only access from the outside was a slanting cellar door opening up in the parking lot. On the other hand, in an adjacent room, a huge furnace boiler, a laundry sink, and a toilet provided plumbing, just what I needed for a darkroom.

Jack Riddle became my client and my landlord. He taught me the advertising business. I sat at his knee each Saturday morning for a year while he schooled me on the business of selling art and photography. We became friends and later, partners. We created advertising ideas, drank bourbon, made bad jokes, worked twelve hours a day every day and screwed the beautiful women who thought we were cool. We admired their good taste. We thought we were cool, too.

Within five years I was at the top of my game, a game I was perfectly designed for. Was I that good? No. I simply was good enough. There were better photographers than me. But I took Jack's advice about charging more. On that first day I doubled my quoted price to $200 a day and that week picked up two assignments. Since anything worth doing is worth overdoing, taking the leap into the unknown, I then decided to charge $500 a day. The clients rushed to pay it, and I hired two more photographers to handle the work overflow.

By then, my partner Jack, in his stylish dark glasses and me in my black beret, owned the largest advertising art and photography studio in five states and when we sold together, we got hired every time we presented; we walked away with the largest and most profitable accounts in the state.

As I look back, the black beret I customarily wore was a bit much. Because I was shooting big view cameras, I was in and out from under a dark cloth many times a day, and a beret was the perfect head covering. But it cost me:

I'm sitting in a young banker's office requesting a short-term loan to cover payroll.

My arrogance is palpable, even to me.

"So, tell me about your business," he says, "How do you make your money?"

"I am a photo-illustrator, and I shoot advertising for the biggest and most expensive clients in the state. I also do work out of New York and Chicago and Dallas."

"Really? So how much do you charge for your services?"

"Seven-fifty a day plus hard costs."

He leans back in his chair and folds his hands across his chest. "Must be hard to make it on seven dollars and fifty cents a day, then." He smiles.

"I'm sorry, I didn't make that clear. That's seven hundred and fifty dollars a day."

His face falls and he sits up and regards me with a long look at my head covering. Long pause. "How old are you?"

"Twenty-four...almost 25."

Another long pause.

"I'm sorry," he says, "I can't approve a loan for you. I don't think you are being honest with me. Thanks for stopping by." And he turns away and hits a buzzer.

As I reach the door, his secretary walks in.

Shocked by his refusal, I stand outside his office door pondering what to do next.

He says to his secretary, "I'm not approving a loan for some kid in a beret who says he makes more money in a day then I make in a week. I'm completely offended. He is an asshole."

That was the moment I knew I had arrived. I bought a white Porsche.

Five years earlier, when I was working to sell my first assignment, the parking meters downtown on Seventeenth Street, the high-rent commercial district of the city, cost ten cents an hour. I didn't have dimes to spend on the meter, so I parked up on Capitol Hill where the parking was free and walked the hot mile down to the cluster of tall office buildings. The perspiration trapped inside my cheap wool suit always soaked my shirt.

My first year in business I grossed $1,100. My second year, I doubled that to $2,200. Then Lady Luck smiled. Landing a regular account with the client who ordered the bubbles photograph, I was eventually charging $1500 a shot. (About $10,000 in today's money.)

But, after eight years of this utterly nerve-wracking, fancy dancing work, my heart begins to murmur.

"Stress," the doctor says.

"You don't understand who you are talking to," I say. "I'm bullet-proof. I grew up rough, and I'm perfectly suited for this trade. I love this business."

"Suit yourself...," he says tapping my chart with his forefinger. "You are thirty-four years old, but if you continue at this pace, at this stress level, you won't reach forty."

"That's bullshit, Doc."

Back on the street, I look at the sidewalk. Fuck you, Doc. Who the hell do you think you are? You don't know a friggin' thing about me.

But the further I climb up the money mountain, the more tired I feel.

Since the terrifying adventure on top of the Wyoming oil derrick, I had produced many dangerous assignments; hanging out of helicopters, airplanes, race cars, off of building roofs, blast furnaces, and the most dangerous of all, beautiful wives. There wasn't anything I hadn't done in the field. Maybe it was time to move to a profession where staying alive was a better prospect.

THE RANCH

Of course, dying at the hands of a young Italian man never entered my mind. The ranch, after all, was just a land deal, just business, just money.

Newly arrived from Denver, owning a ranch in western Colorado seemed like an appropriate ambition for a city boy with Old West ambitions—cows, cowboys, horses, saddles, six-shooters, sunsets, Levis, alligator boots, big belt buckles and anything else that makes up the Western Myth.

Seven hundred and twenty acres of ranch land comes up for sale at a good price, and of a size I can afford—if I can find someone to front the down payment. Inspecting the property on foot, I feel small; in the old west, a man afoot was no man at all. However, at the highest point of Dallas Divide, in the San Juan Mountains of southwestern Colorado, my breath comes short, my imagination fires, my vision of myself grows by a foot, and my eyes fill with tears. Just think, me, being a rancher here above the rest of the world. The Mount Sneffels Massif rises in front of me like a gray, serrated, 13,000-foot wall while the avalanche chutes gouge deeply into the unyielding pockmarked faces of the peaks ranging raggedly to the right and left of that snow-tipped King of Mountains.

My land is mostly flat on top, broken by shallow draws that drift down to the lower part of the ranch and then fall sharply over a cliff, into a creek drainage. Wild turkeys live undisturbed down there, strutting and roosting and cackling, isolated from hunter's shotguns. The dirt road from the highway is gullied from years of neglect and abuse by rainwater and melting snow.

The aspen trees and short ponderosa are thick on the north side of the land where the snow drifts melt last giving the trees an extra week of water each spring.

Otherwise, this is a dry ranch; desert dirt, low rabbit brush and sparse copses of skinny aspen trees struggling to make a parched life, their spidery shadows ragged and crippled against the dead leaves beneath.

The walls of a log cabin stand gray weathered beneath a rusted, corrugated tin roof, the window-eyes open to the vicious weather that can ravage this high world in any season.

The remains of the cabin sit alone in a slight swale among stunted trees and stare blankly out over the verdant and picturesque Uncompahgre Valley a thousand feet below and the blue, high saw-tooth peaks beyond. This is movie country. John Wayne country.

I stand and look at the old building for a long time. I'll rebuild it and use it for a summer cabin. My family can escape here on weekends, and we can sleep comfortably under the rusted tin roof that may leak a little here and there but it'll be mostly dry inside. Some tender attention can bring the log cabin back to life, restored to the tradition of the old west.

The property is a couple of miles from the highway, at the end of a dirt track; only cattle and wild game and the fortunate owners can be here. No tourists. Only invited guests and the occasional unseen interlopers, wanderers curious to see this slice of heaven untouched except by grazing livestock, the occasional deer or bear or mountain lion and the rustic maneuvers of the ranching family that owns it.

Enzo LaBianco, the seller, represents the heirs to this property. His parents settled here in the 1880's. They lived, worked, and died in this part of the county and kept this land for their cattle's summer range. In the fall, they would move the herd down to winter in the valley below. The hollow-eyed cabin is the only evidence of the passing of those adventurous Europeans who civilized the real West. This small log monument ties me to their history, enamors me, makes me feel like the logical inheritor of their work and dreams and a participant in the real Old West. This is destiny. I love this place. I shall own it. The thought makes my heart swell. I take deep breaths of the pure mountain air and feel big, even important, perhaps for the first time in my life.

Working the math is easy. My plan is to negotiate a contract with the family and pay over time, keeping a small best parcel while selling off the outlying forty-acre parcels. That will pay for what I keep free and clear for my own account, a perfectly normal land deal, which profits my rich backer around $300,000.

Since the richest man in Telluride is entirely honorable and trustworthy, he handily agrees with my plan and finances the down payment, $30,000 cash, and signs the note for $30,000 payable in five annual payments plus interest.

The seller and his nieces and nephews live in towns. They have no interest in a ranch in the middle of nowhere. For them, ranching is so yesterday. Rather than herd cattle and live rough, they prefer to live the modern life among neighbors, to go to school, go swimming, watch TV, talk on the telephone, have regular jobs and chase their domestic careers.

I dream of Sunday afternoons when I'll take my wife and kids to the ranch, wander the land and refurbish the cabin. My ten-year-old son will steer my Toyota Land Cruiser though the scrub in low-low gear, creeping through gullies and over this rabbit brush and around that deadfall. I'll watch him love life holding a handful of powerful machinery, his knuckles white, his face a constant grin.

New investors are flooding the streets of Telluride. The area, so long a backwater in the southern Rockies, is taking off so new money arrives in the region every day. Sales are good. The market is expanding, and land prices are escalating quickly. City people love to buy undeveloped land in, what to them, are big chunks. And this is the cheapest mesa acreage around. I'll market the land in forty-acre parcels and sell several of those to people on installment contracts. These land contracts call for a down payment and monthly payments until paid off. After paying Enzo his share, I'll get mortgage releases from him and then I can deliver a warranty deed to the new owner. Again, all standard stuff in the land business.

As I become more successful in the real estate business, I may build a real home here, way above the fray of the modern world, perhaps run a herd of cattle of my own, and live in isolated splendor.

The death of the dream does not come quickly; it is protracted and painful. And dangerous.

First, seventy-one-year-old Enzo LaBianco is stopped over a traffic violation, has sharp words with a state trooper, gets thrown over the hood of his Chrysler, gets handcuffed and ducked into the back seat of the patrol car destined for jail where he slumps over and dies. Heart attack.

Instead of dealing with one amenable representative, now I am compelled to negotiate with his ten young relatives, none of whom I have ever met.

Then the Saudis screw me. They decide that oil is too cheap. Gathering the rest of the oil producing states, they conspire to raise the international price of oil from $3 a barrel to $12 and even higher in the United States.

The western world stops. On a chilly Saturday afternoon in October, 1973, commercial silence falls over the land. Business stops. There is no money. Worse, there are no land buyers or even signs of any. It's like a nuclear bomb has exploded over southwestern Colorado and left a mushroom cloud boiling over my ranch.

I now own a ranch with no prospects of paying it off. Ever. I am totally broke. I stop paying the mortgage note to the family. I stop sleeping and worry every waking moment and every long night, too. There is no way for me to honor my obligations. If I don't uphold my contracts with my new buyers, if I can't get the land out of hock and deliver titles, if I stiff my land buyers, the real estate commission will take away my license and I will have no way to survive. I will have to move my family back to the city. The forty-acre buyers will sue, and I can't blame them. The LaBianco family will sue also. I've sold off several forty-acre parcels that, technically, I do not own. If I lose the ranch through non-performance of my debt with the Labianco family, I will be unable to fulfill my new contracts. I have no defense. The whole pyramid scheme relies on new sales and new money passing through to the LaBiancos. I am trapped between the Saudis, my new buyers, my backer, license law, and the Italian family. Every way I turn I'm in trouble. It can't get worse.

Exactly a year after the oil crash, the annual land payment to the family comes due. There are no land sales to be found anywhere. Within the last month, my wealthy backer died of cancer. His three heirs, now my new money partners, are not willing to bail me out; they are dubious about their aging father's investment acumen and especially dubious about me, the real estate devil who hustled him into this disaster.

The rope tightens. I've lost 15 pounds and hardly ever sleep. How do I get out of this? How do I slip the noose? Step off the trapdoor? Crawl off the gallows floor? Set aside the deal and my inflated ambitions as a rancher?

On payment day, I drive to Montrose to meet with the family to give them their annual payment of $38,000. I borrow gas money for the trip.

I knock on the door of the suburban red brick tri-level and am welcomed into an ordinary living room with brown furniture. Sitting in a rough semicircle, the family of Italians, older sisters of uncertain age and working-type young men and women, smile at me with expectant expressions. We shake hands all around.

I take a deep breath and launch into my carefully designed and rehearsed pitch.

"Thanks for meeting with me," I start. "As you know, this economy has died. The oil crunch has hurt us all and killed business in this region."

Then I hit my persuasive stride. "We have a new survey of your property, that is, our property, and have sold some pieces of it on contract. This year, we sent you about $40,000, and you released a parcel to us. Your family has received all the proceeds of what we have sold so far, so you have done better than most of the people who still have land for sale."

I look around the room, and ten pairs of eyes show me doubt. Considerable doubt.

Pushing on, I say, "Your mortgage makes us partners until it is paid off. I expect to be able to resume our annual payments next year when this Saudi oil shock is over, and the market recovers, which it will. Nobody saw this coming. Telluride and the mountains are broke, but we are all going to make it through this downturn one way or another. Land sales will come back eventually, and your next annual payment will be made on time." It sounded hollow even to me.

Smiling my best smile, I glow over the room.

"Thanks for meeting with me and understanding these regional problems of cash flow."

They stare at me in silence. I turn, pick up my briefcase, walk out and softly close the front door thinking, Jerry, my man, you've done it, avoided being eaten alive by an Italian family. Now, if I can just make it to my car and get out of town.

I hear the door open and slam behind me. I keep walking. At the sidewalk, a hand crushes my shoulder and spins me around.

A young man's face is up in mine; his cheeks are flushed, his right fist is balled into a hammer and his eyes flash pure anger. He has the muscular body of a day laborer. I know he can crush me between his fingers; he has already started with my shoulder.

"Does this mean we don't get our money today?" he hisses.

He squeezes my shoulder harder, and it hurts. I work to control my reflex to dislodge him, to hit him squarely in the mouth. Instead, I steady my voice. "I'm sorry to say, that's right. I have no money to give you."

His eyes cloud over, the lids droop to half, his anger ready to spill into his fists.

"I will kill you," he says flatly.

Fear rises cold up my spine like ice water. I look steadily into his flashing eyes, "Let's get serious," I say, "You have every right to be angry but killing me won't get you your money back. I understand your anger, but that doesn't change the fact that I don't have any money to give you. I am broke. I had to borrow gas money for this meeting."

He tightens his grip on my shoulder. My arm is going to sleep.

"I will kill you," he says softly. There is no doubt in my mind that he means it.

"Your uncle and I made a deal," I say "I can't hold up my end right this minute. He would have understood the meaning of this oil crunch; he was a smart man, he would have forgiven these circumstances. I fully intend to make good every letter of our contract. I just need time, time to work this out and get you your money. Threatening me doesn't speed up the calendar. If you do me in, it will take years to get your money, and you will not even have control of your own land."

His grip barely slackens. "You are a goddam crook, a goddam real estate crook."

He looks away, then back at me. His eyes are red. "Uncle Enzo was a fool. You took 'vantage of him...you screwed 'im...I oughtta beat the shit out of you for that alone. The next time I see you, you better have the money or I will."

He releases his grip and pushes me away. "I know where you live," he says and walks off, his hammer fist still clenched.

I drive out of Montrose, my hands sweating on the wheel.

Driving up Dallas Divide, looking at the spectacular mountains, I contemplate the trap I'm in, between my backer's family and the Italian family. Am I a coward? Reluctantly, I admit that I may be. The threat is a serious one. There is no doubt about that man's murderous ability to pull it off. He won't have trouble finding me at night. Telluride is a small town, and everybody knows where I live, right across the street from the courthouse.

I lie awake for weeks contemplating how to die. Bravely, without a whimper? Staring him coldly in the eye? Rolling over and passively yielding to the murder to come?

How would he do it? Sneak up on me on my way home from the Sheridan Bar late some night? Hit me with a hammer? Shoot me? Beat me to death with his enraged fists? There is no place for me to hide in Telluride.

I tell no one. As the days pass my secret fear grows; it is difficult to think about anything else. What will become of my children? How will they live? Where?

In the middle of another sleepless night a wild thought gallops through my worried mind, I strain to catch its whisper: what happens if I just step out of the deal, give it to my backers, forfeit my piece of it? They have the money now that their father's estate has been settled. And they aren't threatened. I'll just give up, move out of the line of fire, move out of danger. This ranch dream isn't worth dying for. The penalty is too high.

The next morning, I meet the money partners with a proposition.

"I am a terrible partner." I say to them, "I am broke and near bankruptcy. If I BK, that land will be named as my asset and frozen by the court. Everything will stop—sales, money, payments, everything. I would hate to have that happen. Let me give my interest back to you and then you folks are clear of my problems and me. The land is as valuable as it has ever been and you can settle directly with the Italian family."

Reluctantly, they agree. And just like that, the ranch dream is over.

The terror, the exhaustion, the stress, and the notion of becoming part of Old West history, of standing tall on my private cliff looking down upon the most astounding snowy mountain-green valley scene in all of North America, of walking with a swagger, feeling bigger than life like John Wayne, all that is gone. In one pussycat move, my dream of ranching in the Old West ends. Forever.

MC—THE CAT

Once there was this white and very wild cat who was born and raised under my friend's alley shed. My friend lived in a tough neighborhood. I'd been sent home several times from there for being drunk and loud or stupid. Obviously, this cat had had a rough life there among the horny toms and sight hounds; the feline's ratty fur and rheumy eyes were evidence of a difficult life.

A neighbor took the animal home and fed it. It lasted the winter living out of the blowing snow and the brittle up-canyon winds high upon the woodpile under the front porch roof. It was a defensible position, a feline fortress that discouraged the advances of amorous tom cats.

Then the neighbor had to leave for new digs, and the cat had to leave too. Which is how I got the animal: the gift that kept on taking.

When you buy a boat, you get the right to change its name to anything you like. In my opinion, animals are like boats. This cat's name had been Soothead. It was snow white except for a dark place between the ears. I thought Soothead was a dumb name, clumsy on the tongue, non-poetically descriptive etc., so I renamed her Mouse Control, MC for short. (Honestly, this cat didn't give a rat's ass what you called it as long as the food delivery was on time.)

Her former caretaker guaranteed me that MC was the perfect pet: she lived outside, if you forgot to feed her, she would go hunting just like in the old days living under the alley shed. She would pull down a mouse or a garbage bag or anything else edible that was close at paw. Painless ownership.

"Okay," I told her guardian, "I'll take the cat to the Red Farm House with the understanding that this mad killer will manage my out-of-control mouse population. If she doesn't do her duty on the mice, there will be no food from me. I don't need an animal giving me positive feedback to make my life complete and I have enough mice to feed twenty cats. Mice have been breeding in my old house for a hundred years and they have very strong bloodlines and, like all of us here, more than a passing acquaintance with survival techniques."

So MC moved one mile west and came to live in her new home up under the back porch roof with the smelly blankets from her old place and a little ladder to climb home on. Within two days she had explored the surrounding quarter mile on an inch-by-inch basis, creeping through the weeds and around the tree trunks.

On chill mornings, I would check to see if she was still in her new home. She would wake, stretch and kvetch, and demand canned food. Too early for mice hunting season outside.

She got to hanging around the side door, on the opposite end of the house from her carefully customized abode. Whenever the opportunity presented itself, she would look tentatively inside; just looking, like a tourist in a foreign land. Then, one warm afternoon, the door was left open to admit the springtime. She paused at the threshold, surveyed the weather-protected universe contained therein and strolled in just as casually as you-damned-well-please with her fluffy, white dog-chewed tail standing erect, then leveling off suddenly to the horizontal like a prairie thunderhead.

I hissed at her, and her sense of survival clicked in. She spun her feet on the wooden floor, losing traction. Then she flashed through the door and stayed gone for a day.

One morning she was not at the door.

At noon she wasn't there either. I walked out behind the house and heard this mechanical meowing. After some searching, I saw her four stories up in a big pine tree, hooked onto a limb. I talked up to her, but her terror was absolute. Her yellow eyes were wide; she shook her head. She wouldn't attempt the tricky descent.

"Well, MC, I ain't about to climb up there to save your hairy ass. Just be advised that I have never seen a cat starve to death in a tree," I told her. She complained bitterly at my cynicism.

The next day she was at the door when it opened and came through it like a shot. She liked her store-bought food. Later, I found her ensconced on the couch, asleep, her paws pointing to the heavens, her eyes rolled back in seductive ecstasy.

Animals belong outside. I've told that to my kids a hundred times. Inside animals shed on the carpet, on the furniture, and most frustratingly of all, they shed on my expensive, natural fiber, bespoke suits. I have used dozens of rolls of masking tape to lift hair off my city duds. And here was this alley trash sleeping on my green velvet couch, layering it with white hair. I muttered epithets at her but she paid no mind. The Red Farm House was home now, and she casually drifted in and out as suited her perverse pleasures.

One night I returned home late. It had been a long night at the watering holes. I went to the side door which I always left unlocked. It was locked. I went to the front door and then the back door. They, too, were locked. Peering through the window,

I could see Mouse Control in the kitchen cooking something that looked like spinach lasagna. She had on my print apron, the one I bought in Rome. I dug out my house key. It didn't fit. It wouldn't work the lock. I know she heard me rattling the door. She didn't look up, she just kept on cooking, apparently having changed the locks.

I slept in my car and then went to work in yesterday's clothes. Ever hopeful, I drove back after work to find a "For Sale" sign in the front yard. She'd listed the house with a Realtor.

I bought a van.

STORM ISLAND

I up-anchor and join two other sailboats heading towards Spanish Wells. A few hours into the sailing day the wind builds quickly, as predicted, so I duck and anchor in the quiet water behind Rose Island with a few other storm dodgers. As the day wears on, I can hear the wind howl above us, but I am snugly tucked into the quiet lee of the land and glad for that. I've finally learned that sometimes just hanging out reading books until the weather calms down is the best plan.

I lie in my berth and take stock of where I am, and where I was and where I'm going. Am I on a vision quest? Am I attempting to get rewired? I don't even know what the words vision quest mean. Is that someone looking for God? Am I supposed to see the Big Man and discuss politics and my wasted life? I decide that I have no idea why I am here. It's the Zen. I'm here because I'm here. This adventure was just something I made up my mind to do.

I started sailing solo because, after my divorce, everybody else had jobs and women and kids and responsibilities and couldn't get away. I rigged my boat so the two sails could be trimmed from the cockpit and I wouldn't have to bestir myself to leave its safety to handle them. I read twenty books on the art of sailing solo. The pioneers that sailed around the world impressed me. The first American to sail around the world alone was Joshua Slocum in his forty-foot boat. It took him three years and, remarkably, he used an ordinary bedroom alarm clock to calculate the longitudes of his position.

I had no interest in that magnitude of adventure, but hanging out in and around the Bahamas seemed feasible. My boat wasn't a deep keel blue-water boat but a twenty-three-foot lake boat with a retractable centerboard that travelled most comfortably on its trailer. So, I would use that. Yes, it would be tough to steer and keep on course but what the hell, I could do it.

The critical part of sailing shorthanded is self-steering, having a rig that will hold the boat on course without manning the tiller every second. So I paid particular attention to self-steering designs. I built one from a design in a book. It sort-of-worked with a small stay-sail attached to a windward shroud tensioned by surgical tubing. It worked for thirty-seconds or so or until the wind shifted its usual fifteen degrees back and forth, but I figured that gave me time enough to change sails.

Late in the day, as the wind blows hard above us, I decide that a social gathering would break the boredom of waiting for the wind to abate.

I paddle my Jewcanoe around to the largest sailboat anchored in the bay, a fifty-two-foot beauty conspicuously owned by a rich person. Easing up alongside the wall of white fiberglass, I knock loudly on the hull.

A man's face appears above me. "Yes?"

Looking into the sky, I shout, "Ahoy, there!"

"Ahoy back." he shouts.

"We are bored with this weather, and we are putting together a big party for all the boat crews in the bay. Most of us have small boats but we wondered if you would like to join us? You're invited."

"You damned right! We'll be there! When does it start?"

"In about an hour."

"Where is it going to be?"

"You have the biggest boat, so we are going to have it here."

He throws his head back and laughs into the sky. "That's really good!"

Paddling around, I tell other boats about the party on that big boat over there. "Bring a bottle!"

In an hour, dinghies herd around the big boat's sea ladder like suckling pigs.

A dozen sailors stand around the gracious salon, pouring themselves drinks and swapping sea stories of storm death and disaster. Since none of us on small boats have radar, they circle curiously over the radar display.

"That's my boat right there..." they murmur, one by one, as they watch the lighted green circle. The search cursor sweeps around the anchorage creating fuzzy little blips on the screen. "...and there's my boat right there behind yours..."

After an hour or so of drinking and swapping horror stories, partially lit from the drinks, we paddle back to our boats. The wind howls above us unabated, like a freight train rumbling through the sky.

I click on my double-sideband radio and listen through the static to the panicked reports from boats down the island chain caught out in the open water and taking a beating. I look through the binoculars at the horizon; the wave curls out there look like unkempt hair sticking up, jagged, nasty, scary.

I smile to myself. My tiny boat rests quietly. Tonight, I have avoided an argument with Mother Nature. The clouds race above our little sheltering bay and I sleep.

NASHVILLE -TAOS

I'm pretty certain timing is everything and suspected my timing was not good when I happened upon a large group of people standing around a school bus parked oddly on the shoulder of the road. I rolled down my car window and asked a guy watching from the middle of the road what happened.

The man's eyes lit up. "That bus wuz on its way up to the nudist camp," he laughed, "and the driver dropped a wheel over th' edge of th' pavement and the bus jus' tipped over kinda slow like. I uz follerin' and seen th' whole thing."

The bus looked all right now, standing on its wheels, muddy but with little damage. "So what happened?"

"Hell, they uz all nekked in there. The bus sort of laid over, slow like. They all came poppin' out of the door on the back lookin' like plucked chickens." He giggled. "All forty of 'em got under th' bus and flipped it back up on its wheels. Ya shoulda seen it." He was in full guffaw, his face red from the effort.

Driving on, I reflected on the incident and dearly wished that I had been there sooner but that is the story of my life. I am never where the real thing is happening. The really good party was last night and tonight some guy is telling you how wonderful it was and how the women were all beautiful and mostly naked.

Somehow, while I was on my way to somewhere else, Tennessee rolled underneath my van. Nashville is hardly my idea of an exciting place. While country music has come a long way from "You Left a Hickey on my Heart" and "dropkick me Jesus through the goalposts of life" and the "chee-chi-chi-chee" fiddles of my youth, it has never been part of my steady diet. But it was time to stop driving, so I inquired as to where I could find one of those bars with the high-quality southern sound that Robert Altman used in 'Nashville'. I was directed to a joint called *The Stockyard*.

Now, *The Stockyard* was a livestock commission building renovated into a restaurant with an entertainment bar in the basement. While waiting in the foyer for a table, I notice the customers closely scrutinizing the faces of every person that walks in. I realize that they are all looking for a live country music star. Several people actually stare at me. I shake my head slowly giving them the wave off. You ought to hear my Elvis impression, I think. You'd remember it.

A limousine rolls up, and a ripple of excitement moves through the crowd. A lady in a Paris sweatshirt says you can never tell who'll show up at *The Stockyard*. "They show up and jam with each other at least once a week," she says.

The limo disgorges a lovely blonde and her well-dressed date. A sag of disappointment slumps through the gathering. No one recognizes the pair. They look like a married trust lawyer stepping out with his third-floor receptionist.

Out of Telluride I rarely mix with celebrities. We have a deal. If they respect my privacy, I will respect theirs. They do, and I do. Besides, most of the celebrities I have met have capitalized on a single talent. In my opinion, the fascinating people in the world have a number of different talents that they use interchangeably and often.

Earlier in the month, I did run into George Steinbrenner at the Hialeah Yearling Sale. It was a nice affair, and George looked just like he does on TV. He did not speak to me, though. Snooty. The media people call George a sportsman. Typically, the media cannot tell the difference between the guy who hits the ball and the guy who owns the ball.

I could have told those hungry folks waiting to dine with Famous People that none would show up as long as I stood in the foyer. Surely, all the Famous People were here last night.

The girl who stepped from the limo definitely wasn't a star though she tried to look like one; her slick white thigh sneaking out through a slit in her skirt.

After being seated, I thought I spotted Charlie Pride. He looked at me and smiled. His eyebrows went up and he came over as if he recognized me and asked if I would like a drink before dinner. It is not fair to hire waiters that look like music stars.

In the restroom, a well-dressed man introduces himself and shakes my pee hand. He is a City Council Member of Nashville who thought I was someone else. I didn't apologized for his damp mistake.

Downstairs in the bar, the band is outstanding; real Nashville music played by real artists who both start and finish their songs together. The professionalism and presentation are polished show business. The unknown female lead is as good as any voice on the radio. I'm talking to her between sets when an electrical current eddies through the room. A man whispers in her ear. She turns to me, "Charlie Pride is here."

I think it is most likely the waiter from upstairs. However, Charlie Pride is easy to pick out in a room filled with forty white people. It is late, after midnight, before Charlie starts his jam. Pride sings his classic hits, his voice clean and patient. Johnny Russell sings his and on the show goes until closing time. The audience is as mesmerized as they might be at a formal concert.

Everybody dances and sings and drinks and claps at the end of the songs. The atmosphere is fun; just us country folks having a good time.

Last call. The lights come on, and we drink up. I start toward my van knowing I have seen something unique, country western stars singing for the fun of it, a gift to us untalented folk.

I walk up the stairs into the cool dark dawn morning air and nod to a cowboy standing in the doorway in his alligator boots and Indian-blanket jacket.

"Hell of a night of music," I say.

He smiles and pushes his hat to the back of his head with a forefinger.

"That uz nuthin'…ya shudda been ere las nat."

His Indian blanket jacket with the red and black Taos lightning designs and rough, hard weave reminds me that, as a kid, I had one just like it as well as leather cowboy boots with the heels run over so that I walked funny. How old was I then? Six? Eight? I haven't thought about that Indian jacket since it disappeared to God-knows-where.

My father bought the jacket for me in Taos—a squat, dirty little adobe town randomly dropped in a picture book location between the Rio Grande plain and the Blood of Christ Mountains—the perfect place to shoot cheap westerns with no-talent actors and lots of Indian extras.

In those days, everyone called them Indians. That was back before TV and pressure groups made everybody race conscious. Mexicans were Mexicans. Indians were Indians. Tourists were, as always, turkeys to be plucked.

In the plaza, the Indians drank from bottles and quietly talked or stood around wrapped in baby-blue cotton blankets watching the tiny bit of action that went on in the busiest part of town. Occasionally a battered pickup would bounce up against the curb and wheeze silent. And its driver would stroll into the hardware store to buy some fence staples, his beaten slant-heeled cowboy boots making a hollow sound on the sidewalk.

The white man was out of place. It was an Indian and Mexican world, a poor, scroungy, dusty, crack-and-peeled collection of ancient mud huts. As a real place, the culture was uneasy in a modernizing world but it rested more comfortably with its soupy heritage of Pueblo people and natives up from Mexico and the few whites playing out their macho roles as benign conquerors.

Lining the plaza were stores that supported the region's needs with hardware and food and clothes and spare parts. And one store that sold curios.

There was a curio store in every western town then. I never knew exactly what a curio was; it seemed to be those foot-square Indian blankets or the stamped-tin Indian bracelet with the bright turquoise-colored bead stuck in the middle or the buckskin moccasins or the jackets with fringe or little bow-and-arrows you could shoot at the cat. It was junk. Even to a child's eye, it was tourist junk manufactured by white men, trash that the ignorant visitor proudly drove East with. Of course, in those days a tee-shirt was an undershirt you wore under your real shirt.

Now the Indians are Native-Americans. The Mexicans are Hispanic-Americans. And the whites are, as always—the Real Americans. And Taos is the perfect place to visit if you are a Real American.

Today's Taos is a belly-to-belly and back-to-back collection of curio shops, line after line of carefully scrubbed and stuccoed and varnished and painted buildings. Inside each of the sanitized cubes are endless lines of colorful decorations hung on stark white walls. The store managers call these decorations art. The gallery people are as scrubbed and varnished and empty as their gentrified pseudo-adobe cinderblock boxes. There are no Indians hanging around the plaza waiting for the visiting Great Spirit while catching some rays, just Real Americans strolling, looking blankly into windows that tout mounted, matted and framed crafts designed by untalented white people.

Once upon a time, there was great talent in Taos. Now those famous paintings have been exiled to local museums that feature retrospectives or shipped off to Canyon Road in Santa Fe.

Even there, today's Southwest art adheres to the following schools: the Flowing-Hair-Old-Indian school; the Wind-blown-Blanket school; the Horizon-Line school; The Squaw-and-Baby school, the Santa Fe Modern school, the Adobe Churches school and the Frustrated-Housewife-Trying-to-Find-Herself-By-Painting-Flowers school. Each of these formulas can be slightly altered to project a higher consciousness by including a dimly painted ancient vision—a buffalo, a snake or a soaring eagle. Sometimes all three. This kind of other-worldly insight is designed to get the viewer in touch with their spiritual life.

It seems that any curio maker can call themselves an artist if they are physically able to lay down some color, take it to the framer and then cadge some wall-space on the town square. Their product, sold to an unsuspecting tourist, is called art. The place in which it hangs is called an art gallery. None of this is true of course. The gallery is a curio shop. The framed tchotchke is a one-foot square souvenir blanket painted on pre-stretched canvas from Art Mart. The artist isn't an artist but a hobbyist cranking out tiny concepts with a big brush. The Pigeon-

American buys it and takes it back to Minnesota to show her friends the detritus of her tour of the Great Southwest, the Last Bastion of the Wildly Creative Artist. She hangs it over her couch because the colors in the picture match the upholstery. Sort of.

In Taos, there may be three or four pieces of real art, art that makes you think, that gives you new insight, that challenges you to new ways of seeing, that educates you.

Real Americans, that tasteless and ignorant flood, have now drowned Taos. The old downtown is gone away. What remains are parking lots, strolling tourists and block after block of curio shops. There is no local color. The Indians, standing like statues wrapped in blue baby blankets, are gone. No horses or wagons, no hay, no horse shit on the road, no brown children peeking from behind fat purple velvet skirts, and no dogs.

It might have been saved if the locals had only known that geegaw shops filled with paintings of life-that-never-was would eventually displace real life: the hardware store that stocks fence staples, the pharmacy and the place to buy auto parts and a store that sells Levis and pink and blue baby blankets. Maybe if the locals had grabbed the asses of more Texas divorcees with ambitions to paint Indian art; if they had spit snuff-juice on more Real Americans, if they had got a lot drunker and rowdier and a bit more profane; if they had scratched more expensive cars, scared more white kids and raised more hell, they might have a life today in their own charming dusty little corner of the world; a quiet place to sit in a sun-drenched square where barely surviving grass works hard to punch up through the hardpan. Someplace that could honestly be called real.

UGLY BAR

A huge brown doorman in a Hawaiian shirt waves me inside without a second glance. The bar is dark, way too dark to see anything in detail. A radar-scan around the room with an experienced eye tells me that the best seat available is next to the woman with her back to me, the one with the low-cut dress showing a half-acre of beach tan, blonde hair, and flashy legs in spike heels hooked saucily over the brass rail. Just my lucky night—an open seat at the bar right beside a likely slice of heaven!

Usually, I have to scout a room, get the lay of the land and locate the candidates, sort them out and assign a Possibility Value (PV). A PV of 'One' means it is likely I can talk to the woman without her openly insulting my intelligence and that, with luck, I might get lucky, if you get my drift.

A 'Five' means there is no way in hell she'll give me more than a passing hello. She has a rhapsodic body and unaffordable habits like expensive cars, Caribbean vacations, and gifts created from precious metals and rocks. And drugs that make you do weird things without your clothes. In exchange for same, she will bless you with sexual skills that'll make the average man want to start a diary. (At least that's the silent promise.) She's looking for some handsome young devil with swimmer's pectorals, cool blue eyes and money.

This woman, looking away from me, talking to a girlfriend next to her, is obviously a Five. Her skimpy dress is designer expensive, her hair sleek and her calves glisten in that warm wax finish of rich beach huggers. Hallelujah! A break made in heaven! A Five right here at the front of the evening! No working up courage, I'll just barge right in and have an all-or-nothing go.

Once made, the decision instills a fear that another man might beat me to the empty seat, beat me to Five, forcing me to spend the rest of the night angling for position, maneuvering to try to speak to her, my every move frustrated by the intrusive finagling of skillful, lecherous and usually taller competitors.

I walk quickly, actually, I practically run the few steps across the hardwood floor and slither onto the round, vacant, Naugahyde stool. Working to look casual, I order a gin and tonic from the urbane bartender. It comes on a coaster with the bar's name on it. The tall drink feels refreshingly cold as I lift it and drink.

At that very moment, Five spins around and faces me with a huge smile, an ear to ear grin designed to melt the hardest heart and chip the crustiest billfold. The shock of her face jumping out of the dark bar tightens my throat. The gin hangs there and backs up into my nose. I start to cough, hold it, cough again and blast gin all over the front of my white cotton sports coat. The face? How could a face like that be on a body like that? Impossible. Ugly isn't a word; it's a value judgment and, in my judgment, this is one of the worst looking faces I've ever seen.

I look away quickly, avoiding the awful apparition's big black eyes. I spin around on my stool and look out over the rest of the room, along the dark mahogany bar, through the greenery and into the writhing crowd on the dance floor. I can't believe it. Closely inspected, every single face in the room is...well...ugly. Bad ugly.

They smile, they pivot and dance and touch and caress and look deeply into each other's eyes: a happy group, without pretense; a joyfully sensuous gathering of overweight, under-blessed visual misfits laughingly rubbing their bodies together.

Now I have been in polite bars, motorcycle bars, gay and lesbian bars, show bars, sign bars, fern bars and singles bars. There are suburban bars, Mexican bars, porno and redneck bars, above- and below-ground bars, strip bars, star bars, far bars and hair bars but that night was the first time I have ever visited an ugly bar.

And I still can't figure out why the doorman let me in.

ZANE'S BALLS

Beautiful Ariel was owned by this dog named Zane.

He made his ownership clear the first time I met her. The dog stood guard between us, his eyes never leaving mine, his lip pulled back in a permanent, mirthless grin that showed perfect white spikes perfectly aligned to efficiently let blood and tear muscle from bone.

Zane was one-third Doberman, one-third gunpowder, and one-third teeth; his muscles rippled and bulged beneath his hard dark coat. And he was very male. When he trotted down the street, his testicles stuck out behind, as shiny and taut as a pair of baby beets.

He was a machine built expressly for food, fight, and fuck, there was no flee in this dog. And he was never more than a yard away from Ariel. A man on the make had to take his work seriously, for one misstep, the slightest move towards her, the fast twitch of a man kidding around, laughing, being cool, searching for her weakness, one single bad move and you knew in your heart there would be no time for Ariel to scream, "ZANE!..." before he had your head in his jaws.

Hustling Ariel would require discipline. I slowly began to make friends with the dog. A pet here, a pat there. A little scratch around the lean throat bound in strap steel and high tension wire, that piece of terrain just underneath the toothy, action part of God's own killing machine. It took courage. His eyes never left mine except to find Ariel's, apparently looking for some message. I could read his mind: "Is it all right if I let him touch me or should I tear his face off now and swallow it?" He was the most jealous animal I've ever met.

After a while, I took to liking Ariel a lot. She was delightfully smart and both sophisticated and naive, a charming combination. Her straight dark hair, dark eyes, and zoftig build gave her an openly sexual look. Not being terribly subtle, I took that to be a welcoming combination. Zane didn't. Unless locked in a side room, he was always between us. He watched me every minute. His legs quivered. He growled when we hugged. He growled when I pet Ariel. He growled and stepped forward when we laughed. Sometimes he'd growl, bare his teeth and run up and bump my leg with his nose. It was utterly unnerving. One has to be real horny to stand that kind of tension.

Shortly before my time, in a fit of pique, Zane ate the guts out of Ariel's brand new Saab, a college graduation present from her rich and proud grandmother. It had barely five thousand miles on it when one night Ariel decided it would be most pleasurable to spend the night with a new young stud. At his place. Zane, locked in the car, his woman staying with a strange man, experienced an emotionally stressful evening.

Exhausted from an eventful night of familiar drugs and experimental sex, Ariel returned to find that Zane had eaten all the headliner and the insulation, all the door trim and seat upholstery down to the wire frame. It lay on the floorboards in color-coordinated chunks glued together with vomit. He had chewed it, swallowed it, glass insulation and all, and then purged it. Over and over. And over again.

So she drove around in this pristine new car sitting in a plastic lawn chair with shortened legs that she'd lashed into place with the seat belt. The door levers were open to the air, and the steel roof was gray inside, bare as a washtub, with its ribs showing. In a rainstorm, the tin roof drumbeat made conversation impossible.

The Saab was like a Wall Street banker, expensive and polished outside and empty inside. I rode along sitting straight up in the passenger's plastic chair, keeping my hands in my lap; there was nowhere else to put them.

Patience and perseverance will pay off. After dinner and wine, we return to Ariel's little house and Zane meets us at the door like an anxious parent, panting, drooling, quivering and showing his stiletto teeth.

I say, "Can we put him in another room. He's worse than another boyfriend." She giggles, "Oh, of course." She pulls him through a door and closes it softly behind her. "He's been known to open the door," she says with a sly grin.

She turns and says firmly to the door, "Stay, Zane! Stay!"

And then we have a glass of wine. Or two. The TV is on, the sound off, its blue flicker the only light in the room. We don't need lights to do what we are about to do. Nor do we need clothes. In minutes we are naked in the dark making the most enjoyable and primitive of moves.

My naked bottom is in the air, and I am doing what, in my humble opinion, I do best, when I hear the door click open and claws rattle on the hardwood floor. Instantly, the dog is across the room and, with a soulful howl and an awful snapping of teeth, he hits me in the bottom.

His cold nose is like cold steel. The thought of those teeth so close to that nose and that nose so close to what makes me a man sends a chill into the center of my immediate universe. I try to run, to get my arms and legs to work together, to stop screaming. But nothing works. I can't get traction on the same couch that just a moment ago had seemed so righteously full of traction. My feet are pumping—I feel like the track star I have always wanted to be—but all I am getting is upholstery burns on the tops of my toes.

Zane's howls turn into angry staccato barks. His close, hot breath warms my ambitions to leave. After several failed attempts, I finally take the shortest way: over the back of the couch and airborne through the front door, completely naked.

In the suburban street, headlights spot me before I can duck into the bushes.

"Jesus, Ariel!"

"What?"

"Throw me my clothes!"

She starts to giggle, "Come on back in. He won't hurt you."

"Dammit. That's not funny," I whisper, my body jangling with shock. "He scared the hell out of me. That dog is a killer. He is a menace to society. I hate that jealous sonofabitch. He doesn't have any manners at all."

She brings my clothes outside and presses her lips together to stifle her mirth.

In the bushes, I dress in seconds flat. I weigh my choices briefly, very briefly. Her high-pitched, almost hysterical laughter rings in my ears as I start my car after I made damned sure the doors were locked.

THE KISS

My New York City date was a writer with comedy credits, a famous TV series now in syndication among them. She was smarter than me, attractive, Catholic, and by her own confession, totally confused and intermittently suicidal. We hit it right off and spent our first evening together in a snazzy place in the Village, overlooking both the river and the expense. The evening concluded with a peck on the cheek.

Our next meeting entailed an early dinner at the Carnegie Deli on 7th Avenue. The best deli in New York, she said. Her opinion was obviously shared by other citizens since the place was crowded, loud, and full of folks speaking Hebrew. We discussed writing and the writhing that went with it. We discussed telling stories, how lonely a craft it was. And frustrating, too—last year she had a year-long project turned down by ABC. We talked about her problems with the stock market and terminal melancholia, subjects of fascination and delight to me since I am burdened with neither. After her rejection from ABC, she had jumped in front of a subway train. The police were very upset with her. They took her downtown and scolded her with an arrest.

Warming to the potential of a physical liaison between us, that date ended with a kiss containing a fervent wetness that began to smack of intimacy. Brief but promising.

The next try was a bomb. She told me to meet her at the Museum of Modern Art. I was careful to arrive a few minutes early, waiting on the steps of the museum only it was the Metropolitan Museum some twenty-five blocks away. We did not meet.

The next morning I apologized for being a fool. I was additionally angry with myself because I had entertained thoughts of sneaking this lady off for an afternoon of delights.

Third date: we met at the Metropolitan since I already knew where it was. She said to meet her on the steps. In the taxi, I'd visualized myself there, waiting, a lone, mysteriously romantic figure, standing like James Bond in the afternoon light, singularly outlined against the mammoth gray stairway looking like a men's magazine illustration for aftershave lotion. When I arrived, there were 1500 people milling about, smiling into the sunlight, scarfing up the junk food New York is famous for, watching each other watch each other eat.

My date picked me out of the crowd like a skillful cutting horse, and we set off on a breezy, sunlit walk through Central Park. Wearing a tailored suit and a man's fedora, she looked the part of the successful big city woman. We rented a rowboat and floated into the sickly green water of Central Park Lake. It was a scene from one of those cheap little movies directed by an effete New York director who lives with his mother, has never been anywhere else, has no story to tell and damned little budget. I sat on a forward thwart and watched the oars dip while she rowed: Ms. Cool playing boat motor. She liked it.

In the middle of the lake, she said, "Come and sit by me." It was an order. I stayed in the bow of the boat. I don't take orders from anyone except cops.

As evening came on, we strolled down toward Times Square. The bright neon signs glowed, pandering sexuality all over Broadway and its crowds of the curious and kinky. We walked the gauntlet of voyeurism, giggling like teenagers, hugging against the night chill. On a busy corner, we caught a kiss in the glowing half-light.

That kiss held the promise of a passionate evening: long, lingering and enjoyable. The tourists gawked, the locals ignored us. As we walked, the hugs became more intense. She had her hand in my back pants pocket and squeezed my butt for emphasis when she wanted to make a point. Her points seemed to be coming more and more often. Beneath the scaffolding of a building under renovation, she pulled me back into the dark recess of a doorway and began to kiss me deeply and passionately, her hot tongue flashing into my mouth. I happily reciprocated.

Then she latched onto my tongue, sucking it deep into her mouth, and held it there. My tongue was extended so far out of my mouth that the cord beneath it was stretched tightly across my sharp bottom teeth. I felt them cutting into the cord, cutting into it deeply. Pain flashed through my passion and I tried to get my tongue back. This was how I discovered the tongue has no muscles for retrieval. Once your tongue is out there, it is gone forever, if the person holding it won't let go. She was not about to let go. Her heat became more intense as she held my tongue immobilized with suction. I was dumbstruck. I couldn't scream. I couldn't withdraw. I couldn't hit her. I could only wait for her wave of passion to subside. I did moan, quite a little bit in fact. She took those low sounds as encouragement and she went on, sawing my tongue across my teeth. I would moan, she would saw. Moan. Saw. Moan. Saw.

Time stopped, and panic set in. Maybe she was having one of her bouts of terminal melancholia. Was she committing suicide by choking herself to death? By taking me with her? Was there such a thing as an oral death grip? How long would it take them to find us? If I was still alive, how could I explain to the medics what the problem was? Who would they cut to separate us? Would I be accused of murder? Would the National Enquirer publish photos under the banner "TOURIST KILLS COMEDY WRITER IN BIZARRE RITUAL!?"

Then she took a deep breath and suddenly, it was over. My teeth came out of my tongue, my tongue came back into my mouth, and I was in control again, bloodied and shaken.

I sent her home in a cab.

I ta'k'd 'ike 'is fo' ays.

NASSAU CHANNEL

At dinner in the Chub Cay restaurant, the woman is still in tears dabbing at the corners of her eyes. She looks at the man across the table and hisses loudly, "You son of a bitch! I hate this, and I hate your friggin' boat and I hate this place." She dabs at her nose and clinches her hanky inside her fist.

As the tableau unfolds, it seems that in the middle of a rough squall, the inflatable dinghy they were towing flipped upside down and went pearling, that is, dove underwater. Acting as a sea anchor, it stopped them cold and made their boat unsteerable. In a storm without steering, they were at the mercy of the merciless ocean and any disaster that could happen predictably would. So, in desperation, the skipper cut the Avon loose and they watched it pop to the surface then flip end-over-end downwind from wave top to wave top and disappear into the spray. Gone forever. Flotsam.

"If there were a way to get home I would go home right now," she says angrily; her jaw muscles work. The man looks into his plate and grunts.

"That dinghy cost us over a thousand dollars!"

Her face is set in the horrified expression of the terrified sailor, at that moment when cold fear turns to hot anger. Everyone in the room empathizes with her. We've all been in that place where money counts for nothing and survival counts for everything and the remembrance of stark fear triggers anger. The room falls quiet except for the after-sniffles of the distraught woman and the clink of forks against plates.

"Sailing is for fools," she says into her food. Her voice is flat. "I don't know why I put up with your high-horse captain attitude and your damn boat, barking orders at me as if I was a damn slave. You are having a great time but all this sailing does is scare me to death. And you turn into a living asshole as soon as you step aboard that damn boat!"

Her voice drops but the timbre of it carries across the room. She sniffs, "You sold a perfectly good airplane for this white walrus! It's the dumbest thing I've ever seen you do. Dumb!"

He looks into his plate and eats.

At other tables, women's eyes are cast down into their plates and heads nod. Men watch the angry woman sideways and smirk. I feel relieved that I am free of that kind of conflict.

The following morning breaks clear and breezy. A Nor'easter has moved in during the night, beginning with a few introductory puffs then producing a steady ten knots here at the docks. Since yesterday, the wind has clocked around to the north, so I have the wind on my port side and a beam reach, a perfect point of sail for my course southeast to Nassau.

The day looks good, but, physically, I am beaten. Exhausted. Every movement requires concentration. Effort. Discipline.

Rather that sail out to the channel, I start the tiny Sears engine and motor out by the moored boats. As I putt along, all I want to do is lie down in a quiet bunk and sleep for a day or two. If I get to Nassau, I'm going to do exactly that.

To conserve my energy, I have learned not to crowd on sail just to gain a little bit of speed but to keep canvas reduced and the boat riding more comfortably. When the wind speed increases just five knots, the pressure in the sail doubles. Too much sail aloft can cause knockdowns: the unexpected puff of wind that overpowers the sail which slaps the boat onto its side until the lee rail goes under and water fills the cockpit. Unless sail pressure is released, drowning follows closely. As I move out of the lee of the island and into open water, the wind hits at least twenty knots and quadruples the sail pressure. I am surprised at how hard it is blowing out here. The boat jumps violently in this almost-visible wind. Ahead, I see the waves whipped into white horses, a daunting preview of adventures to come. This is going to be a rough day. But, if I get into the Nassau channel, protected from this northerly, I can rest.

My boat isn't built for heavy weather sailing. It is too light, too fragile, too bouncy and beats the crap out of the skipper. I trim to balance sail and tiller pressure and stand in the cockpit with one foot down on the lee rail, the tiller between my knees.

Then the puff I dread comes, the air thrums loudly in the rigging, the mast points at the horizon, the boom and mainsail drag the water, the lee gunwale submerges and the ocean waterfalls into the cockpit. The now horizontal sail floats on the surface then begins to fill like a bathtub, the accumulating weight holding it down. The overpowered rudder comes out of the water, loses its grip and the boat goes out of control. She violently rounds up into the eye of the wind. In a tired slow motion, I pop the mainsail sheet out of the cleat and release the wind pressure on the over-stressed mast and sail. The boat slowly stands up, gathers herself, and shivers to a stop. The sails pop loudly and flog in irons.

In the books I studied, the message I took away from the single handers' high adventures was that the enemy of solo sailors is fatigue which develops into the inability to make decisions, into craziness. Of course, they are not talking about me. I have never had trouble making decisions, even wrong ones. And I don't go crazy. But, in a number of cases, in mid-ocean, around-the-world single handers simply swam away from their boats toward some imagined island, to disappear forever, their ghost boats found drifting months later. In one case, the sailor would jump off his boat under full sail, let the boat slip by him and then catch a line trailing off the stern, pull himself aboard and repeat the swim. Obviously, if he missed grabbing the line going by his face at ten miles an hour, he was lost forever. That was the thrill and a way to pass the boring job of sailing across the ocean alone.

The wind gusts are increasing which means that I must go forward and shorten sail, drop the jib on deck, then shorten the main. To do that, I must unsnap my safety harness from the lifelines, haul myself out of the safe cockpit and expose myself to the wildness. But I can't seem to move. Maybe if I wait, the wind will diminish, and I can avoid going to the bow. I just can't go up there right this minute. I'll wait to see if the wind drops.

Another knockdown and the boat reacts violently. I'm immobile. Frozen in the cockpit. I have nothing left. Empty, I can't think, and I don't really care. Living or dying makes no difference anymore.

Another knockdown. My boat is struggling. Detached, I watch the movie from the back of the house. The mainsail is in the water, and the belly of the sail is filling, adding weight, each wave becoming an anchor holding the boat on its side.

Another knockdown. God I'm so tired. Bubba, you are a pussy. What happened to your balls? I can't move away from the tiller. What if I die out here? What is happening to me?

Street Hustler cheats death again and again over the next few hours, all in slow motion. And I don't care if the boat breaks from the strain. She lies down, nearly drowns, stops, shivers, then, once again, haltingly stands up on her own. I watch it all happen through a distant fog. Survival now depends entirely on the boat recovering herself.

I stare into the scudding clouds. How fast they are moving, how white, how startlingly bleached, how fluffy the zoo full of animals they shape, how beautiful this natural poetry filled with graceful graphics, a series of moving photographs showing in the salon of nature. I want to remember this day, to keep it imprinted on my mind. This is my last day. I feel it.

My girlfriend is here beside me, her high school smile and smooth thighs…we're necking in the front seat of my old Chevy at the drive-in theatre…the velour upholstery rubbing my knees raw…the warmth rising from her body smelling sweetly of passion…wait!…what the hell are you thinking?…she has been gone for years…married some guy…had a baby. No she hasn't; she is still here with me, on the boat, right beside me holding my drink, smiling at me, giggling at some bullshit story that I can't remember now…was it about cats?…something about her damn cat…Callard is here, too…standing right in front of us…he's laughing and saying "….after all I taught you, you really are a pussy… you're out here and ready to die?"…he is angry… "get a goddam grip!…pay attention!" I say "Okay…" aloud; then he dissolves into white space. I stare at where he was, I turn to my girl to tell her that Callard was right here talking to me and he is pissed off. She is gone, too.

My vision clears back into focus. The boat, the sails, the ocean, the sky, the wind. I can't die out here…that would be damned lonely…Bubba, where is your brain?…where did it go?…where has it been?

Slowly, the hard decisions I must make come into focus: tie off the rudder so it can't move, let the boat naturally go into irons, let the wind back the mainsail, unsnap my safety harness; leave the safety of the cockpit, crawl forward where the motion is wild and dangerous, allow the boat to drift in the froth of the whitecaps and wander and flog and flail at the mercy of the wild wind and angry seas like a drunken dancer.

Callard...I'm better'n you think I am...I am more of a man than you think...you told me once that fatigue makes cowards of us all...I am tired but I am not a coward...I'll show you...I got the balls...I got a pair...

Quickly, I release the jib sheet which snaps violently and the sail beats, cracking loudly in each gust. Then I unhook my safety harness line and crawl forward along the bouncing deck, pull the jib down hand over hand and secure it to the lifelines. The boat rounds up into irons, the sail cracks and pops, the jib halyard shackle strikes snake-like, raps me in the forehead and then tries to blind me. The boat, now free of control, bounces and yaws wildly. I spend at least half my energy gripping a lifeline on this bronco ride, sometimes suspended in the air, sometimes pressed to the deck, twice my weight. I try to yield to the random wildness, not to resist it, to accept it. Lying on my back I wrestle with the sail. It wants to belly up and blow over the side. Fighting the billowing nylon, I finally lay on the ballooning fabric with my whole body and bungee it to the lifelines.

I crawl hands-and-knees back to the safety of the cockpit where I shorten the mainsail and sloppily tie off the clew to the boom leaving a big wrinkle up the belly that spoils its shape. It makes no difference in this blow; spoiling the shape of the wing slows everything down.

Back in the relative safety of the cockpit, with my knees forking the tiller, the boat now responds to my steering. With shortened sail, she rides smoothly up this wave and down that one. I'm glad the trip forward is over. I am so tired my knees shake. Everything is blurry. My head hurts.

Blood drips off my hand and smears on the deck. I've hurt myself, but I don't know how. A glance tells me that the cut isn't deep; I curl the flap of peeled skin back to where it used to be; I have no memory of banging something.

Three miles from the Nassau channel entrance, I am surprised at the stately procession of sailboats marching from the south, huge racing sails parade along the horizon. Oh, I remember now, Miami radio tells us that the Southern Ocean Racing Conference is in its annual race from Miami to Nassau—maxi-boats and twelve-meter racers on the rich man's annual hunt for glory, expensive compensation for their big egos and small appendages. In this race, glory is the spice of the masculine ideal, pitting Goliaths with big clubs against Davids with small stones. Everyone in that club wants to club the competitors.

The entrance to the Nassau Harbor channel is narrow, and I approach it with relief. I need rest; I'm going to lay up here for a while. My mind is going away again. My body is tapped out. I hardly have the strength to stand. I press my hand against my side to calm the shaking.

Steering into the harbor I can see the town low in the trees, with boats anchored along the shoreline, their hundred masts appearing like a stand of slim reeds. I look over my shoulder; a large boat is overhauling me to the leeward. I hold my rudder steady, and she silently slides by, a dozen feet away to starboard, her fifteen white-uniformed crew at their stations all peer down at me. What are they staring at?

Watching the boat, elegant is the only word I can think of: seventy feet of a stately seagoing woman, sensuous, sexual, white, gorgeous. Going away, her name is gold leafed on the fantail: *Windward Passage*; the emotional pet of a wealthy man. I envy that guy, and I envy any boat that can survive the fickle whims of the deep ocean.

In Nassau, I can anchor close to the quay because my boat hull is shallow. At sundown, I jump into the Jewcanoe and paddle the few feet to shore and tie up with a gaggle of other dinghies.

In the nearest bar, I find myself hanging with various SORC racing crews. Beers abound and talk is loud. Across the room, I see the 'Mouth of the South," Ted Turner, holding court among sailors. Having won the America's Cup and, burdened with Southern humility, he doesn't let anyone forget it.

I say hello to a man who could only be crew for one of the racing boats. He is big, obviously a grinder, one of the musclemen who physically crank the winches that trim the huge sails on racing yachts. His shoulders are massive, the muscles in his forearms bulge, his blond hair is close-cropped, his face tan, his eyes blue—a perfect Nordic specimen of Superman. He towers a foot above me. The beer bottle is small in his hand.

"Which boat are you on?" I ask.

"Windward Passage…"

"Oh, you guys passed me in the channel entrance…incredible boat you guys're drivin'."

"Yeah, it is. What boat you on?"

"I'm on Street Hustler."

he laughs. "We saw you. You're the guy we passed in the channel aren't you?"

"Yeah. You folks blew by me like I was standin' still."

"We saw ya. You looked like a goddam dead man on a dog leash with your safety harness and all. And your main had a wrinkle in it like an old carpet. Whatcha been doin'?"

"Well, I came over from Lauderdale and went into Grand Bahama and then down here."

"Who came with ya?"

"Nobody. I'm single handing."

"In that little boat?" He looks at me sideways, "How big is it?"

"Twenty-three feet..."

He looks across the bar and is silent for a moment, "You did the Gulf Stream in a twenty-three-foot boat?" He chuckles.

I nod.

He stares at me, shakes his head and says slowly, "I'd never do that...it's...too...fuckin'...dangerous... You, my man...are crazy as hell."

He shakes his head again and walks away. I watch his huge frame move back to his shipmates. I feel foolishly macho. God, the victories out here are small.

HARVARD

The dining hall at Harvard University is exactly what one would imagine: full of big walnut trim, big paintings, big space, muffled talk, a steam line with overdone veggies and unidentifiable meat courses, thick bulletproof china plates and cups that are dangerous when thrown.

At meals, students are encouraged to sit with strangers in order to learn about other peoples' lives, to broaden their experience. Sitting across a table from two average looking women, a mother and daughter team, after the where-are-you-froms and do-you-have-familys, I'm asked the third predictable question:

"What do you think of Harvard?"

"Oh, it's okay. There are things about it I don't understand."

"Oh, such as?"

"Well, this place is supposed to be the best America has to offer, yet…"

The daughter looks at me askance.

"…people here don't laugh."

"What do you mean, they don't laugh. We laugh all the time."

"I've been here for a week and people here seem to be very serious about life and everything else. Where I come from, we laugh all the time."

"And where is that? Paris?"

"No. Telluride."

"Never heard of it."

"It's in Colorado, in the high Rockies."

"Is it one of those ski places?"

"Yes."

She tosses her head disdainfully.

"Well, we laugh here all the time," she says with finality.

Minutes of silence follow with dedicated attention to the French fries. The awkwardness is broken by a muffled laugh somewhere in the vault of the hall.

The mother's head snaps up. "See, we laugh."

The next day I join a young man who is lunching alone.

"Hey," I say, "How're ya doin'"

"I'm doing fine, thank you very much." He doesn't smile.

"May I join ya?"

"Of course."

Long silence. The hall resounds with clanging trays and banging dishes.

"Where ya from?" I ask.

"Boston."

"Whereabouts in Boston?"

Without looking up, "Back Bay."

"Wow. From what I understand, that's a really cool place."

Coolly, he looks at me. In a condescending voice he asks, "And where are you from, might I inquire?" His tone implies 'West Jesus.'

"Yeah, you can inquire. Telluride, Colorado."

His voice is oily, "Never heard of it." He speaks slowly as if to a backward child, "I'm sure it's lovely for you."

"It's a little town in the high Rockies, southwestern Colorado."

"I suppose you eat a lot of corn and beans way out there."

"Don'cha ya eat corn and beans here?"

He literally looks down his nose as he says, "My mother's table was covered with exotic vegetables...kale, kohlrabi, mustard greens, purslane, and asparagus."

"In the West, we're meat eaters, deer, elk, bear, buffalo. And we have a delicacy you don't have back here—pika. Ya know what pika is?"

He draws back as if assaulted, "No."

"It's a small furry animal that lives high in the mountains above the tree line. Lives under the slide rock. Only us locals know how to catch 'em and cook'em. We just gut'em, hammer'em flat, dip'em in pancake batter and fry'em for two minutes a side. Eat'em with fried Navajo bread."

"Don't you skin them?"

"Oh, God no! In tha hide'n hair, that's where all the flavor is, delicious. If you are ever in the West, be sure to try pika. You'll never forget it."

He shivers. "How do you spell that animal's name?"

"P…I…K…A. Fuzzy little animals."

If there was ever a workaday guy miscast as a writer it is me. My last course in English was Littleton High School in 1954. I had to leave because I made trouble for everyone. After writing stories for a decade, I've decided that I am grievously unqualified to be a writer. I know nothing about diction or story architecture or parts of speech or sentence construction, I only have the arrogance of ignorance which allows me to write stories unencumbered by the technical details of the English language. Thirty-five years after Littleton, I realize that my reach exceeds my grasp by several orders of magnitude. Therefore, I am stunned by my acceptance into the English Department at Harvard Summer School.

Walking to my first class on the main campus, the one with the big library and the statue of John Harvard, I look at John's statue and try to read the guy. He doesn't look like a party animal. I make up my mind on the spot: "I ain't goin' drinkin' with you, Buddy."

I ask my way into a classroom that looks like a million others worldwide. The woman professor is attractive with a nice face and an easy voice. I like her. At a break in the teaching action, I slip her a note:

"You are a gorgeous woman and I would be thrilled to take you to dinner this very evening at your restaurant of choice." She reads the note, takes a careful look at me, smiles, and drops the note in the wastebasket.

"I take that as a no," I say.

She laughs. "No, but thank you. Are you in this class?"

"I think so. I'm supposed to be in basic English."

She shakes her head. "You are in the wrong room. Your classroom is in the house on Mount Auburn." And so it was.

Eight of us sit in a semicircle on the battered second floor of this beat up old house. Six are young. Two of us, a local housewife and I, are long in the tooth.

The instructor is a faint little guy whose claim to fame rests on his published novel (*published!!*—as an actual hard-bound book for crissake!) about the fraught relationship between his mother and his aunt: parlor fiction, chick lit.

The class drill is write a story a week, and hand out a copy to each student for each week's free-for-all critique.

Now, critiques at Art Center, my only other school experience, were simple: I come into the classroom, place my photography assignment on the blackboard rail and then sit back without comment while the classmates beat the fraud out of my brilliant concept. No mercy was ever shown nor asked and that was the value of the school: they called bullshit wherever they saw it and taught all of us to do the same. We were training to be professionals and they treated us as such. It was a scarring experience, one that enabled us to penetrate the fraudulence and rationalization that is systemic in creative endeavors, to explode the vaporous fragility of ideas.

Our second class meeting in the old house entailed critiquing a story written by the housewife; a story about her brother, a sociopath, and how he had screwed up the family.

The criticisms go around the room. They are light and accepting, even polite, and the author nods appreciatively. At my turn, I do the only thing I know how to do: offer an Art Center critique, cutting through the language screens, euphemisms and sisterly tenderness, directly to the muscle and bone of the story.

When I'm done, there is complete silence in the room. Looking up from my notes, I notice tears in the writer's eyes. Then they overflow.

"This is my story, not yours!" she screams. "Write your own stories! I've read your story and it's terrible!" She yells into a handkerchief, "Leave mine alone!"

The next afternoon my school mail box contains a letter from the instructor:

Dear Mr. Vass,

Because you are so intimidating and outspoken a presence in the classroom, please refrain from participation in the story critiques.

Thank you for understanding.

(s) Derek McMillan, MFA, PhD
English Department

I am not especially surprised by this limitation. I have been advised countless times throughout my life that my comments and opinions were out of line, out of the mainstream. In other words, best to keep my mouth mostly shut.

In intellectual paradise I am a stranger but I want my friends and family to understand where I am, not just Boston but Harvard! So, I buy Harvard sweatshirts for my entire family (and me), the ones with just the word HARVARD written in a big maroon arc across the front and the logo VE RI TAS.

I had been assigned a corner dormitory room in the Dunster House, the building with the red cupola that faces the Charles River and symbolizes this historic school. Here, a view of the Charles River begrudgingly reveals itself as a vertical vision of paved street, half of a tree, a brick wall, a pie-slice of sky, and the occasional jogger flashing through the narrow slot.

Now, my house in the San Miguel Valley, while ancient and not very clean, had a certain pioneer log-cabin panache, an implied century-old comfort for its occupants. This dorm apartment is simply shabby; showing the wear of rich kids without respect for anything that came before them, kids who grew up with old cracked leather and Chinese Red wallpaper. A paint job would have helped this place but it couldn't cure the wear and tear from the abusive years of kid rambunctiousness. A single bed, a table and chair indicate the spare institutional budget but I don't care. It's better than a sleeping bag on the ground freezing my ass off, which I have done for too many nights of my life. It is cool outside but this room is hot and sweaty.

I want to do what a regular student does. I ain't ever been to college before. I'm fifty-seven and this is a one-time event for me. I have never just sat down in one place with my sole job being to write stories for the educated people. The prospect is daunting. I've only ever written for ordinary folks, in the Telluride Times, where my pieces were printed adjacent to the real estate ads. Oh, every now and then I got a subhead under the headline, but that only meant that there wasn't enough news—an additional line fills the white space.

Sitting in a hard chair in a dingy room in historic Cambridge, at the oldest university and home of American gentility, wealth and political power, trying to create a story to write as a school assignment, I come up with exactly…nothing. Nothing! Ideas, when they come flitting through my mind, pop like soap bubbles immediately upon touching the pointy reality of the keyboard. I stare at the gray screen of my Macintosh for hours, repeating "Ya gotta think of something, Bubba. Ya just gotta."

Then a solution comes to me: watch television. I walk around to the cut-rate store and buy a small black and white TV and tune into the Senate hearings starring Oliver North as he reveals that Ronald Reagan lied about international double-dealing.

That eats up a couple of hours. Then I take a run along the Charles and watch the racing shells, their extended oars dancing together to the beat, looking like water bugs, touching the surface gently, leaving rings behind, the crew bending as one. I listen to the coxswains bark their count. Another hour gone.

Sleep might help.

Lying on my pitifully thin mattress, my mind drifts and I find myself thinking about my daughter Roz. God, I love that girl. Very smart. And she is me. More than me. Smarter than me. I am disappointed with her boyfriend but we all have to play the cards we're dealt.

Suddenly I think I can write about that. Where does the story go? What's the arc? I'll work that out as I go. It's a love story. Love always wins, that much I know. It will be a happy story. It can be anything at the beginning and the middle but it must end with everybody happy.

So I write this:

> A LOVE STORY
>
> A squat, middle-aged man sits against a palm tree. His belly hangs over his swim suit. He watches a young woman stretched motionless in the noonday glare. After a time she stirs and sits up.
>
> "Okay," she says hazily, "I can't take any more of this. I'm going back to the room." In a smooth motion she unfolds her lean body, sweeps up the

towel, shakes it and walks down the beach, her hips rolling, adjusting to the soft sand.

The man heaves himself up and follows his daughter, stretching his back as he walks. "I'll go with." he says. "It's too damned hot. Besides, I'm bored."

The fraudulent coolness of the motel room envelopes them. The woman falls full length onto the bed with a small groan. The man sits heavily on the other bed and the springs complain.

"You seem to be off your feed, Babe." he says.

The woman looks at the man sideways over the top of her arm, her eyes worried. She breathes deeply.

"Bobby," she says quietly, "I'm late."

"You're always late," Bobby says. "You were born late and you've been late ever since." He giggled at a memory.

"No. I mean I'm late with my period." She watches him carefully.

His salesman's smile stays. "Which period? The period after your name? Rosalind Period. Drop the period. Make it a silent period." He chuckled. "How late are you?"

She closes her eyes, "Three weeks."

"Aww...three weeks." He smiles. "Listen, I've been around women all my life and for a girl like you to be three weeks late is nothing to worry about. At your age you can be late from puppy love or running a stop sign... just about anything. Don't worry about it."

She sighs, "I'm worried about it."

Bobby smiles showing teeth. "Well, who's the lucky father?"

"Martin."

"Ma-Ma-Martin?" Bobby shakes his head. The girl's boyfriend invariably stuttered when introduced and Bobby invariably calls him by all three names. "Ma-Ma-Martin? You slept with that dimbulb? You know, I love you a lot, Roz, but except for me you have terrible taste in men. What the hell do you see in him, anyway?"

Her voice gets hard. "He makes me laugh and he doesn't hassle me."

"You can do better than Ma-Ma-Martin. He's an airhead."

The surf-beat drums on the door. The air conditioner hums a counterpoint. The man looks long at Rosalind. She slides down off his lap and gallops across the yard, her little dress flying and flashing frilly, white cotton panties—even at four she has the sassiest little bottom any father has ever seen.

"Ma-Ma-Martin, huh? So, you really don't know or not, is that what I hear?"

"No, I really don't know. But I feel rotten."

"Physically?"

"Yes, physically."

Bobby throws his hands up. "OK...well...we just can't mope around here without knowing for sure, can we? They got those pregnancy test things that you work at home... you know those?"

"I've seen them. It's worth a try."

The man lies back on the bed and spreads his arms like a crucifix. "We'll get one after dinner. It is worth a try." In time, he snores.

In the drugstore he smiles at the package, holding it up and turning it over under the icy overhead light. "You read that one and I'll read this one," Bobby says and hands Rosalind the box. "This one says it can tell after only three weeks if you are preggies. It's got yellow daisies on it. Cute."

Quickly, Rosalind puts hers back on the shelf. "Let's do that one," she says.

"When I was a kid this was all done with rabbits, ya know. The rabbit had to die. If the rabbit died you were in trouble and you had to get married."

"I know," she says curtly.

"Hey Babe..." Bobby says brightly, "...this ain't the end of the world. Lemme tell you about some of the scariest times of *my* life."

Rosalind looks away, rolling her eyes.

"When I was in high school I thought I had this girl knocked up. Scared me to death. I was scared for weeks." Bobby takes a deep breath and smiles mischievously. "But she wasn't. I had all that fear for nuthin'. A lot of life is like that...fear over nuthin'. The best way to beat fear..." he doubles his fist and shakes it slowly, "...is action. Action conquers fear. That's why we're going back to the room, have you whiz in this test tube and see if the little brown circle shows up that says you're gonna be a proud mother."

"That sounds like a ton of fun," Rosalind says.

"It won't, ya know — show up I mean, the brown circle. Some mushrooms maybe..."

She smiles but it fades, "Please, this isn't a joking matter."

"Hey, little girl, you're damned lucky to have me around. Most fathers would go nuts if you sprung somethin' like this on 'em. We've been together too long to fight over somethin' silly like this." He touched her on the cheek. "I'm on your side, ya know."

The test tubes and chemicals are spread out on the bathroom window sill. Bobby peers up close, through his half glasses, as if searching for the center of the universe. "Can you see anything in there, Roz?"

Rosalind comes into the whiteness and puts her face close to the test tube. Their heads nearly touch and Bobby smells the female in her hair. He slides his arm around her waist. She is taller than he remembers. Focusing through his glasses he inspects her closely. He squints to see her nose and cheek and lips and the soft fuzz on her ears and her hair sun-faded metallic.

She used to be so small, he thought. At the dinner table her feet didn't even touch the floor. She chased the dog and squealed and went to school in long dresses and braided her blonde hair and played with dolls and hugged her daddy.

Rosalind shakes her head slowly, "I don't see anything yet. The directions say let it sit for thirty minutes."

"I told you there wouldn't be anything; let's give it some time to work so we can settle this thing and get back to our vacation." He laughs nearly up to his eyes. "I can't take the pressure of all this. I'm going for a walk."

Bobby steps into the liquid air. The salty wind has freshened and the surf is rowdy. He walks up the dark, empty street and stops under a plumeria tree. In the glare of the streetlight he fingers the wind-nervous pink blossoms. Fallen blooms litter the ground.

God, she's a big girl now, he thinks, a grown woman.

Holding a petal between his thumb and forefinger, his head droops. She used to be so small. So innocent. So fragile.

Acid tears blur the edges of his eyes. Finally, they squeeze out; the colors on the ground dissolve and run together, flowing like beaded glass.

"God, I feel so old," he whispers. Slowly he sinks to his knees, his shoulders hunched against the wind, his fists clenched against his mouth. And he sobs without a sound.

On the second floor of the old house, it is my turn in the barrel; I have submitted my story and the full semi-circle is armed with academic knowledge.

"This story is not believable," says a fresh-faced English major with authority.

"Why do you say that?" the professor asks.

"Because no father would never talk to his daughter like that. No father ever would treat his daughter like that, speak to her like that."

The housewife says, "Besides, this man is a pervert. The reference to white panties and her butt are the signature of a child molester. This guy is a child molester!"

Half under her breath another student says "…and it makes me wonder a little bit about the writer."

All the heads turn and look at me. I turn my palms up and look back. Their eyes drop.

Someone says, "Who would trust this narrator?…he's a salesman for goodness sake. You can never trust what salesmen say. This story uses an unreliable narrator. I can't believe this story because it could never happen the way the writer tells it…never in a hundred years. Would you trust your daughter with this pervert?"

I start to giggle behind my hand. It is muffled at first, eventually breaking into the hooting, awful, blackboard-scratching scream my laugh dissolves into on those rare occasions when it flies out of control.

The semi-circle doesn't crack a smile.

At that moment, I knew my career in academia was over. I would never be a writer like these people were: correct, acceptable to society, with perfect proper diction, sensitive to the educated sensibilities of the upper classes who own this place, its philosophies and its very thoughts: where everyone wants to be Walt Whitman.

That afternoon I packed my Subaru station wagon and readied for the road. My very last act was to stop at the Harvard

University Book Store and tip every book on writing into a shopping cart.

What did I learn in Boston? I discovered that when I sit down to write, I can screw up with immense and perfect confidence, even authority. Being ignorant is not a burden for me any more. I can look down my nose at the poor uneducated masses, josh them about their primitive diets, talk very cool at parties about Ivy League schools and bodice-ripping fiction. I still don't know a gerund from a Geraldine but I can fake it now, like many other college grads. Now I speak with the authority of the credentialed: I have attended an Ivy League University.

FLY UNITED

Denver to Chicago is a jaunt across town, an air-taxi ride to work and I have done it often. Occasionally there may be weather or equipment problems, usually nothing critical. It is a workday business, check in, wait. Board plane. Wait. Takeoff. Wait for the gong that releases you from your seatbelt. Study the research for this training assignment. Business flights are airborne study halls.

Before we leave the ground, some guy standing above me in the aisle wants my seat.

"Are you in the right seat?" he asks.

"Yep, here is my ticket," I show him my boarding pass, "Obviously, they've double booked the seat," I say, "Go see the flight attendant."

He approaches the attendant, and they hold a brief whispered conversation. The passenger is moved up to First Class. The pretty blonde stewardess immediately blesses him with a professional strength smile and then plies him with strong drink. He is happy.

I am unhappy. I like First Class; the food is better. With a slight change of timing, it could have been me up there flying with people that bathe regularly and speak in complete sentences.

Three-quarters of the way into the two-hour flight to Chicago, the captain comes on the speaker, with his granular voice doing his best to sound like Chuck Yeager. I pay little attention. I've heard a thousand schticks from wannabe stage actors turned airline pilots. Out of the corner of my ear, I pick up the weather report for Washington, D.C. This pilot loves his theater and is dallying on the loudspeaker, giving us more information that we can ever use.

I turn to the very middle-class lady beside me and ask casually, "Where you headed?"

"Charlottesville."

"By way of Chicago?"

"No. Washington."

"Oh."

I order a gin and tonic. Pondering the possibility that this lady is on the wrong plane, I feel sorry for her. Certainly, her people waiting in Virginia will be disappointed when she doesn't show up at the arrival gate and learn that she is trapped in O'Hare.

The guy across the aisle looks like a friendly sort. Even forgiving. I touch him on the arm.

"Where is this plane headed?"

"Washington," he looks at me suspiciously, like I am a terrorist. I do not look dangerous. It confuses him. "Why do you ask?"

"Just checking up on these airline people. You never can tell when they are going to screw up."

He squints, "Where are you headed?"

"Uh... Washington I guess."

I lay back in my seat. How could I get on the wrong plane? This takes me back to the first grade in a new school. I am in the wrong classroom, dumb and disoriented, with not a friend in sight. Suddenly nothing looks familiar: strange plane, strange people, strange sky.

I turn to Middle-Class Lady. "I'm on the wrong plane."

She smiles. "You are not serious?"

"Yes ma'am," I tap my watch. "I'm supposed to be in Chicago about now."

She starts giggling. The man by the window starts giggling. The man in front of me giggles. The man across the aisle watches suspiciously for hidden weapons.

"What are you going to do?" the lady asks.

"I am going to stop this plane...I'm getting off."

I walk aft and find the stewardess puttering in the galley. "I'm on the wrong plane. Get on the radio," I say, "and book me the first flight back to Chicago."

When I return to my seat, the whole section is sniggering and bobbing their heads and looking at me sideways. I bury my nose in the inflight magazine. During the last half hour I fake sleep. You can't be too cool.

At touchdown in Washington, the stewardess comes and speaks in a voice that carries well above the engine noise. "You depart through the rear door," she commands, "there is a van waiting to take you to another United flight. Hurry, you have two minutes to make it." More snickers. Laughing eyes meet mine as I run the gauntlet, toting my bags back through the plane.

A grim passenger agent stands propped against the rear exit hatch.

"Are you the guy that got on the wrong plane?"

"Yeah. The passenger agent screwed up. I got to get to Chicago to work in the morning. I'm the star. I gotta be there."

He looks at his watch, makes a face and looks at me.

I say, "I guess this happens pretty often, huh?"

He gazes at me over his nose. "No," he says.

We dive down through the hatch and into the waiting van parked on the runway.

The tight-lipped driver is silent as we careen across the rain-enameled runways of Dulles International. I think, this is just like being caught in the wrong kindergarten class—and I know from experience that while it may take weeks, even months, eventually the embarrassment will go away.

CHICAGO

I rarely carry cash, preferring traveler's checks, but while working in Chicago, I get a pair of hundred-dollar bills from a client. Stuffing them in with the small folding money I have left, I walk to my van which is parked on the street. It's a gorgeous afternoon in the South Loop and the skyscrapers cast long shadows over the traffic.

Approaching my van, I notice a huge black man dressed in a powder blue polyester jumpsuit walking away carrying a bicycle just like mine. It has a tool kit just like mine. His arms are full. He walks slowly and deliberately south on Franklin Street. He is carrying a music system just like mine, too, and the speakers, and the shortwave radio and the tiny TV. Obviously, this behemoth has excellent taste in consumer goods.

In my pinstripe suit and wing tips I trot up to him, "That's my stuff," I say. I don't feel angry; just a bit frustrated that sometimes, in this world, one's stuff is hard to hold on to.

He stops and slowly turns, looking at me through chemically glazed eyes. This druggy could get hinky, I think. Adrenaline rushes through me.

"Is this yo stuff?" he asks casually, "Let me give some of it back to you."

He hands me the amplifier and the bicycle. It is all I can carry. He'll unload his arms, put the rest of the load down on the sunny sidewalk and walk away, I think. But he just keeps ambling up the street carrying the loot. He doesn't look back.

I look down at my suit, pristine in its establishment statement. I look down at my shoes, newly buffed by a man with natural rhythm in the Sears Tower. I decide on the spot that bullet holes or abrasions in the dark British Super-150 fabric would be undesirable. The shoes were made to look expensive, not made for running. The hell with it, I thought, he can have it all.

Stomping back to the van, I open the cargo door and throw the bike and the amplifier inside. I lock the door even through the vent window is punched out, its pieces a handful of paste diamonds on the driver's seat.

By now, the big man is a block away hailing a cab and out of my reach even if I were silly enough to challenge a drugged-up black guy who outweighs me by a hundred pounds. Fat chance, I say to myself.

A gruff voice behind me says "That mofo got yo stuff, man?" He was also a black guy but smallish, my size, in a black beret and a worn combat jacket with battle patches.

"Yes, sir," I answered, "That mofo done hit my van." (When in Rome....) He gazed at my banker's suit, sizing me up accurately as a businessman-coward.

He takes off running at top speed toward the giant who is now loading parts of my life into an idling cab at the curb. The little man jumps into the cab's backseat, following the big man. The taxi doesn't move; its door hangs open. This has to be the slowest getaway in history. Of the three people so far involved in this robbery, I seem to be the only one under stress.

Slowly, the little man backs out of the cab, followed by the armload of my goodies. He casually strolls back toward me, his arms full. As he approaches, he smiles. "Dat mofo didn't want to give it back… I 'most had to cut'im."

Down among the loot, he is holding a knife as long as a man's hand and shiny-shiny. Its pointed malevolence makes the adrenaline pump in the back of my thighs.

"I am really impressed," I say. I spread my arms wide and embrace the air. "I'll take care of you for this."

He smiles at my reaction to his violent world. "Jus' a little somethin' would be awright." He carefully stacks the equipment on the van floor and turns, holding the knife as casually as a toothbrush. Digging in my pocket, I come up with the folded cash from my pocket. The two hundreds come out on top. I had forgotten them. Surprised, I flip by them and by a ten-dollar bill and then stopped at a twenty.

"Here," I hand him the twenty-dollar bill. "I just want to thank you. That was a helluva of a thing you did there."

Holding the hundreds, I watch the blade. He watches my money. Neither of us moves. Time hangs by its second hand.

Finally, he looks up at me. "I thought I uz gonna haf to cut'im," he says again with a lopsided smile.

As he disappears around a brick corner, he looks back and actually laughs at the honky in the custom suit and alligator shoes.

ENRON TAKES THE BULLET

In the fall of 2001, Enron, the hottest company in America, their stock a flyer, was in trouble—management chicanery. Enron approached Dynegy Inc., a competitor, to save them from collapse. My assignment was fly to Houston and help the PricewaterhouseCoopers Transaction Services Team (a fancy title for the merger and acquisition consultants) design a presentation to be made to Dynegy that would take advantage of the uncertainty created by Enron's meltdown and get PwC hired to replace Andersen Consulting as Dynegy's consulting firm. It was a classic business move: kick the competition while they are down. On this ordinary Tuesday afternoon, November 26, 2001, there is no hint of what tomorrow might bring. I have a meeting with the Houston boss of the M&A guys who reiterates the layout of the deal they are working on: PwC will replace Andersen as Dynegy's consultants and help Dynegy buy the sickly Enron.

The target is Chuck Watson, CEO of Dynegy, and the size of the deal is $10 million a year in fees repeated over five years, a fifty million dollar hit.

Here's the playing field: Enron is already in that critical area between dying and death. As a last desperate tactic, Ken Lay, Enron's chairman and CEO, approaches Dynegy's Chuck Watson. His proposition? Merge their firms and save Enron. Chuck Watson, in typical Texas cowboy style, with no due diligence or investigation, quickly shakes hands with Lay on pursuing the deal. He plugs in $1.5 billion of Dynegy's money to keep Enron afloat until the merger is finalized.

Enron's stock is at $4.11 and trembling, down from $83.

Chief Financial Officer Andy Fastow's chicanery is all over the television; he is accused of off-books tomfoolery and self-dealing, a fancy word for stealing from the stockholders. He has been fired along with his cohorts but the Street has lost faith in the entire firm and is showing no mercy on its stock price.

Andersen Consulting works for Enron in the dual roles of auditor and consultant for $137,000 per day. Andersen approved the Enron managers' tactics to create off-balance-sheet entities—phony businesses—to hide losses. Andersen signed off on those special transactions to make losses invisible and the members of Enron's board of directors, who trusted their advice, are now in jeopardy. Everyone is dizzily spinning in the whirlpool. The SEC is on the prod. Stockholder lawsuits are being filed every hour. My client, PwC, says that on this very day there are 245 lawyers working on the Enron-Dynegy deal.

While Andersen Consulting has yet to be charged with wrongdoing, they have a history of pushing the envelope of regulations with other clients. The SEC settled with Andersen for illegal actions involving another client, Waste Management. Their liberal, even illegal, interpretation of regulations in favor of their clients gives Andersen an unfair advantage in the marketplace and has created hard feelings between them and their competitor, PwC.

My client's brief explanation of how they will approach the presentation to Chuck Watson is technically mind-boggling. I know from past experience that these consultants know too much. They won't easily divorce themselves from their education long enough to get the deal done with Watson. Unless we rise above the tech talk, it will be deadly boring for Watson and he will ignore this world-class opportunity. It's my job to simplify very complex material for presentation purposes. But I expect only limited success in prying my client's hands off the shovel handles of their intricate knowledge and getting them to focus on digging into what interests Watson. It will take some serious reformatting to get the presentation on track and keep it there.

I think about a risk management approach. Since much of high level consulting is about managing risk, I ask what Watson's risk tolerance is at this moment. My client is unable to say, so my initial idea goes down in flames.

That evening I walk along Smith Street by the Enron Tower with its big stainless steel E logo at the front entry. I look into the dim sky and the lighted windows checkering the blue-mirror glass of this modern monument to free enterprise. It is hard to grasp the idea that the slick Texas giant hanging over Houston's downtown is severely, perhaps fatally, wounded and that this iconic building is now a hollow shell of free enterprise, the husk that remains after crooks have gnawed the ambitious guts out of it. Tonight, there are people working hard around the building. I watch the neon-colored lights in the logo chase themselves like pachinko balls from the top to the bottom and then disappear. Just like the billions in cash that have passed through the firm. Tomorrow morning this real estate will be fully populated again by scared and confused and angry people.

While my first pass at the presentation plan has failed, it still seems to me that the plan is the most logical; the risk is all Dynegy's, now a reputable firm with a high stock price. It can get dirty hands playing with Enron, and that should be the theme of the presentation—managing the risk to Dynegy's image; the risk of losing total credibility on Wall Street, thus hurting its stock price. It is quite possible that if the Enron disaster is large enough, (and right now there is no way to tell) everything and everyone around the deal, culpable or not, will emerge tainted in the mind of the public. A tainted image means falling trust and falling trust means falling stock price. Once a stock begins to plummet there is a fair chance it can fall to worthlessness. It happens quietly every day in the market, mostly unnoticed by the public and the media, who specialize in happy talk. Happy talk is where the money is made. Creeping disaster makes unhappy talk and scares investors away.

So, that's the story I'll help PwC create: Chuck Watson can distance himself from Enron and stay clean by hiring PwC to replace the tainted Andersen Consulting. In synch with that, PwC can launch a loud public relations campaign to create space between Dynegy and the malefactors at Enron even while saving the sick company from certain death. It would be like performing heart surgery on a dying patient using a long scalpel to avoid getting blood on your hands. Difficult, but it could be done.

The next morning, November 27, I am waiting in the client's office. I drink coffee and read his Wall Street Journal. I have been making notes since yesterday from TV stories on CNBC and tearing out printed articles about Enron. There is no good news. According to the talking heads, everyone in the firm is a motherless, money-grubbing thug.

My man never shows up.

At 9:30 I meet with my real client, the western regional director of the M&A line of business at PricewaterhouseCoopers. He is a friend of our little training business. He is an aggressive and fine salesman, a rarity at any professional services firm.

Inside the conference room, the table seats twenty people or so. A north wall of windows looks directly at two tall buildings diagonally across an intersection of Smith Street—the forty-story Enron Towers. The new building on the left is just being finished and nearly ready for Enron's occupancy. There are still windows blinded by plywood eyes and scaffolding stacked down low. This pair of shining monuments is joined by a raised walkway that circles over the intersection itself. The Enron buildings, seen through the big windows of this office conference room, seem near, their architectural presence reflected in the dark, deep finish of the huge wooden table.

Around ten o'clock, a slim man in a white shirt walks in and scratches "$2.97" on the whiteboard. Without looking at the people circling the table he turns and leaves silently.

After a pause, staring at the whiteboard, my client tells us that he has assembled his various specialists into a buyer team and a seller team and after we decide how we are going to format our message, they will role-play the presentation around noon. Then, later in the day, they'll call Chuck Watson, walk across the street to Dynegy's offices and present their plan for the salvation of 20,000 Enron employees.

Consultants wander in and out. They carry a rumor that Enron will file for bankruptcy on Friday, the day after tomorrow.

I watch the role plays. The PwC teams are anxious to present their technical expertise but they don't seem ready to close a deal, the hard, scary part for technical professionals. I explain how the presentation pieces should go together and the mindset of how to tell the story of keeping Dynegy clean by hiring our people. Drop the tech talk. I use a 'bloody guy in the street' analogy—you come across a man bleeding badly, lying on the sidewalk. There is no time to get acquainted, to schmooze, to build a relationship, to explore credentials or to explain your process to keep him from dying. First you must simply stop the bleeding. You'll get to your credentials and complicated medicine later.

They agree to my opening premise, "Help Dynegy create ten billion dollars over five years without getting dirty with Enron."

Dynegy is Andersen's client also. I say, "Andersen is tainted and obviously tainting their client in the eyes of the analysts. There will be repercussions on the street."

A general nodding of heads, agreement all around.

Now it's 11:00AM. I'm meeting with the presenters: the three big PwC bosses— the structure expert, the tax maven and the energy trading expert.

I can barely tolerate the hour of discussion about technical stuff, arcane accounting concepts developed precisely to confound the ordinary unwashed like me. I suggest to my man that this technical stuff is moot, that the technical expertise is a given, expected from a firm like PwC, the largest consulting firm in the world. The real issue is keeping Dynegy clean by firing Andersen and hiring a new firm, creating distance for PR purposes.

I don't feel that I am getting through to these people. We seem to be passing like ships in the night.

Sometime before noon, ENR stock falls to $1.20. The New York Stock Exchange suspends trading immediately,

At that moment, Moody's re-rates Enron bonds, downgrading them to junk. Their bonds are now worth twenty cents, down from a buck.

The media is having a field day, hysteria floods the airwaves. The money honeys are working the high drama into a sexual lather. The bond rating downgrade triggers $20 billion of instant debt, as the collateral for the many loans that Enron has made contains stock price limitations, that is, price triggers. If ENR's bond rating falls below BBB, it trips the triggers and the loans are immediately due to be repaid…not this month…not this week…today! Today is the day a huge chunk of cash is due because Moodys has lost trust. It means that borrowing becomes an instant distant memory for the firm. Life support systems have been unplugged. Cash is oxygen. Now, we get to watch the patient die a gasping death.

My client buys into the idea of distancing Dynegy from the Enron demise.

There is no change in the room as the head of Transaction Services Global walks in. Now there are three other bosses in the room. There are soft hellos around and the discussion continues, everyone working to adjust their ideas to the changing circumstances, searching for solid ground upon which to format a presentation that fits the exploding bits-and-pieces of the train wreck now rolling toward the inevitable plummet off the bridge.

A telephone rings. Transaction Services is on the phone with the London PwC office. The UK branch tells him that this call is for PwC's internal use only and not public information. He listens and nods without speaking. He clicks off. And then, in a quiet, ethereal voice, he says, "Enron UK has just announced that they are insolvent. Their insolvency announcement has triggered action in our UK branch to handle their insolvency action. Our London people are working on that now."

Someone softly drawls, "Jeeeesus…" The curse hangs in the air.

There is a long break in the action. People occupy every chair around the tennis court-sized table. They are slumped along the walls, standing half in and out of the doorways, leaning back into the whiteboard, silhouettes against the picture windows. The day is gray with low clouds and the room, weakly lighted, is somber, moody, set dressing for the down and puzzled mood. People look at the table, or out the windows at the low sky, or at each other.

Now the kings of the arcane—the lawyers—are in the room and for an hour there is a discussion amongst the Office of General Counsel, 'on the other hand' arguments about the proper position and ethics of presenting to Dynegy. The consulting bosses, the auditors and everyone else have opinions, since all consultants opine professionally and each must have his say or they come down with a touch of nausea and a sick headache. There are many comings and goings, huddles and rump meetings and phone calls, whispered conversations and a snow flurry of obscure words and acronyms.

I look out the window at the polished Enron tower disappearing into the fog. I study it, wondering who will occupy it, which firm with hundreds of worker bees who think too much and create what they believe are genius ideas and spend most of the day acting like they are working.

I go to the men's room, then to the coffee room. I stand and watch CNN. The TV image is bright and exciting. The sound is low but it doesn't take long to deduce that Enron is the lead story and that this video segment has been looping for a while. The talking heads are not sure who is hurt because of the derivative positions held by outside players. But this much is sure: Chase and JP Morgan are on the hook for heavy bread. Their stock will drop, too. Everybody who played with Enron is now getting mud on their pinstripes.

Around lunchtime someone sets a laptop in the center of the conference table. People huddle around the computer staring. It is quiet. They watch ENR's real time stock quotes. The price line trending down. One can feel the losers inside the lighted screen holding their breath. It is a miniature theatre of the absurd.

I elbow into the huddle like I'm joining a crap game. Mesmerized, we all watch Enron's stock fall out of bed. It is horribly fascinating, a company dying instantly but in slow motion. We watch the dissolution of someone's idea of a great idea, the disappearance of millions of hours of sweat equity, thousands of people's lives, the death of ambitions, self esteem, kid's educations, retirement funds, marriages and, in at least one case, life itself.

Enron stock had been $83 last year, back when life was good and the bookkeeping was bad. But that ogre of business, the destroyer of ethics and the good life—hubris—came to play, took over the game and pumped the ball too full of hot air. When it exploded, the shrapnel killed every hope, and every accomplishment, everybody.

In the huddle: ENR 80 cents, then 76…74…71…77…oh good, it's recovering a little. Somebody is buying, trying to catch a falling knife. 72… Whoops. 71…71…71 cents. The ticks are leveling. There is hope. 71…73… Then 70…69. It looks like the small investors are bailing out. At this rate of fall, certainly the large investors are bailing, too.

Then—capitulation. 60... Even the bottom disappears from view. Twenty people sit utterly silent. Another fifteen lean against the walls looking at the carpet.

Finally, "Well, that's it. We're done," someone says.

No, I don't think so.

To the client I say, "The stock market reacts like a hysterical woman. I'll bet DYN is being pulled down by this. Tainted."

Someone from the huddle clicks to a quote box and enters DYN. It has fallen 10% in one hour.

The tax guy says, "Chuck Watson is in for one and a half billion on a hard pipeline asset. That part is real. If Enron bankrupts, he can win. Or with a straight buyout he can win. Enron has no chance of redemption in six months. Actually, whether he planned it or not, it's a great deal for him."

Someone mentions Enron's energy desk.

"It's history," I say like I know what I am talking about. "The energy desk has no assets beyond computers, software, people and the trust of its customers. This collapse is an extension of the dot-com bust. The energy desk has no underlying value beyond the brainpower of the people. That may be good for business but it's bad for bankers. Now they are only going to probe for hard assets. Dynegy, while a rival, is not in the information business, they are oil and gas guys."

The energy mavens say, "Nah, Enron's energy trading operation is a valuable asset."

I say, "It's not a viable asset even though it was the biggest income flow Enron had. Trading is built on trust. When trust leaves the market, everything of value leaves with it."

I realize that these true experts are humoring me, being polite and professional and correct and that, compared to their knowledge, I don't know jack about energy trading. It dawns on me that while there isn't a lot of animated conversation in the room, it is chockablock with brilliant people in tasteless neckties. And I am swimming alone in the deep end of the pool.

Hangers-on overflow into the conference room and spill out into the hallway. Standing, slouching, looking at the floor, out windows, preoccupied. In all of business America, this is the one place to be on this grim morning.

Someone says through the open door, "Chuck Watson is giving a web cast to the stakeholders right now." Somebody reaches over and punches up the laptop. Total silence in the room, vacant eyes fixed on the screen.

A PwC guy says, "He's going to announce that he's got a billion and a half in it and he's taking Enron out of bankruptcy."

Watson's tinny voice from the tiny computer speaker scratches around the room. Instead, he says he is rescinding the Dynegy purchase contract with Enron, using the "material change clause" to escape. He says, "We're all right. Our market is all right. We are protecting our stockholders. By doing this we have protected ourselves all the way around." He clicks off.

The predicted scenario is wrong. I can feel the disappointment; the room is crestfallen. Nothing is going right. No plan is working. I keep hunting for the large issues around which we can format a presentation. This is my third try today.

Another hour of discussion on conflicts of interest and what we can do about them. There is consensus that we can't make a move without creating conflicts.

People offer a flurry of guesses about the technical aspects, burrowing down in the mechanics of DYN's need.

I finally stop it again. "Sirs, this is speculation of what to do if you get the account. Right now, we don't have the account. What Dynegy needs is image rebuilding by an untainted, brand name consulting firm." Grim nods around.

From up against the wall, someone says, "We need a meeting with Watson."

Now we are getting somewhere. Action conquers fear.

I say, "Who is gonna make the call?" I expect a half dozen voices to volunteer. This is the chance of a whole lifetime career, to count coup, to walk into a flaming building and pull 50 million dollars out of it without even getting singed. Who in business could restrain himself from at least trying it? Think of the glory. Think of the reputation. Think of the money.

Frozen silence. The room is Antarctica.

After silent minutes, my man says, "I will."

People began to speak up. "Whose account is this anyway? How can we call on this account if Bob owns it? This is his account. Where is Bob, anyway? Why isn't he here?"

"He is on a plane somewhere."

"Then we can't call Watson because his primary contact is Bob. He's been working on this account. It wouldn't be ethical."

A lawyer says, "I'm not sure we want to do this at all. There may be risks to the PwC partnership."

"How long before we can define our risk?"

"A few days…perhaps by Monday."

A manager shakes his head, "I'm going to call somebody." He walks out.

We resume developing the opening move, setting the scene for the assignment. We come to "Help Dynegy rebuild its image on

Wall Street, insulate it from the merger debacle and recover its stock price." Agreement around. Heads bob.

"Now that you are going to get hired…" I say, "…what are you going to close the engagement on? What job can you get started on immediately that will move them toward protecting their stock price?"

"We could do a pro forma," someone says weakly.

"OK, good. The time is now. Quick. Move quickly and boldly. We can do this!"

There is silence. Every eye is focused on me, the presentation expert. A modicum of enthusiasm floats in the air for which I am thankful. In this single moment I have earned my consultant's fee.

Murmuring approval, people head for the door. Chairs scrape, people smile and leave along with the three bosses, the energy guy, and me. Together, we five stroll back to the manager's office.

We hang around the desk. These are seriously smart faces figuring the next move. I'm ready to design the presentation, commit the moves to writing so these experts don't mess it up and look like fools.

They talk. Yes, we can do this but we can't do that. This is a big ship. There are lots of moving parts. This move on Dynegy is an ethics mess, a can of worms. It is a debate. What can be done? What can't? We can't say bad things about Andersen even if they are idiots. Who's on first? What's on second?

I am at the end of my patience. I look down the long hall lined with cubicles on each side. It is a foreign land. I'm trapped in desert sand surrounded by deep pits of regulation, ethics, expertise, hesitation, indecision, risk aversion, arcane knowledge and internal political maneuvers.

I think: This firm is so big and so smart it is muscle-bound. It is a giant brawny wrestler with bulging muscles, heavy brows and a great tan. But it can't move; it has no athletic ability, no flexibility. For this firm, there will be no kazanga leaps from the corner post to the center of the ring. Bubba, you are an idiot for thinking you could ever pull this off.

So, we stand around talking small waiting for the manager's return call. It never comes.

Near dark we all leave the building. The fog has turned to rain. To me, the wet street is fresh and simple, the pavement real, the buildings shiny and aligned along some predictable pathway toward a simple life. Cars spray and people slosh along, heads down, going home, back to where life, even if not simple, probably does not require backbreaking effort to march in place. On the horizon, I can see jail time for the Enron managers.

I send PwC a bill for $15,000.

They pay on time as they always do.

BIMINI

Approaching Bimini from the west, I sail out of the startlingly deep, blue Gulf Stream onto and over the edge of the table-top that supports the island chain. The water in the ocean-river between here and Florida can be four thousand feet deep. If this river bank, this uplift in the ocean floor, was twenty feet higher, the entire Bahama bank would be dry land, a flat desert country. On the top of the table, Bimini pokes without drama through the surface, flat and green with buildings white and square turning scarlet in the sinking sun.

Near the harbor entrance of Alice Town, I hold to the channel and steer for the bluest water as the ocean here goes shallow deceptively fast, changing hue from blue-black to deep cobalt to turquoise to white where the water is two feet deep.

A hundred yards from the entrance, I look down to watch the fish dart away from my passing shadow which crosses over a twin-engine airplane completely submerged in a dozen feet of water. A Cessna, perfectly intact, its white wings and Plexiglas cockpit wavy images in the surface ripples. Tomorrow morning I'm going to come back here and dive on this wreck to see if there is something worth salvaging.

After tying up at the dock and giving the native dock-master his fee, I walk down the simple wharf, find a bar that overlooks the harbor and sit with a warm beer watching the fading light.

After dark, I stroll around the small settlement. At the edge of a cluster of houses tucked under some palms sits a ramshackle house with an open door. The light from inside outlines what looks to be a child in a thin dress, with flowers in her hair. From out of the dark a mature woman's melodic voice calls to me.

"Ere's bootiful girl jus' for you, sir."

I don't answer.

"Sir, this bootiful girl a virgin."

From the road, I look carefully at the girl. The backlight of a bare hanging bulb shows skinny legs through her thin dress and outlines her coltish body leaning fetchingly against the door jamb, a child trying to act sexy. Bobby socks with lace tops catch the light. The child awkwardly beckons to me and smiles uncertainly. The warm breeze in the palms rattles the fronds above the shack. I walk up to her. Her feet twist in black Mary Janes.

"How old is she?" I ask the dark voice.

Her black face comes into the light. As she speaks, her big smile shows the deeper blackness of missing teeth, "She be sixteen on she a virgin."

I try to see the girl clearly. Even in the backlight the girl's tan velvet skin shines with sweat, her eyes glow dark brown, her smile shows young white teeth. A mulatto, she is certainly the issue of a black woman's service to a white man. This woman's baby?

A picture of my daughter flashes across my brain. Leaning over, I speak softly to the girl, "What's your name, Honey?"

"Marietta," she says with a smile and looks away at the dark woman.

I say, "You shouldn't be doing this, Marietta. This is not good for you."

She nods and smiles uncertainly. Her eyes cut to the woman.

"How old are you right now?"

Looking at the ground she whispers, "I be sixteen."

The woman says, "She love ya, sir...she make ya come...she twenty dolla." Her smile fades. "She good...she a virgin!"

"Marietta, how old are you, really?" I ask.

Twisting in her black school shoes, she hesitates, then, quietly, "Thirteen."

"I love you but not tonight, Dear," I say.

I shake my head at the dark woman, then walk back to the road and away.

The dark, edgy voice yells after me, "Sir...fifeen dolla."

In my berth, I can hear a plane approach the island. Landing in this moonless dark at a sandy airstrip without navigation aids has to be high adventure; there is no room for error. This afternoon I sailed across the price of that error.

These islands are the drug frontier. Drugs flow into the States along this island pipeline from South America, pumped north through the chain by airplane and boat. The thing I most fear is to turn a corner into a small channel and interrupt a drug shipment being manhandled from a slow trawler onto Cigarette Boats that then roar to Florida at eighty miles an hour. The lawlessness of this country puts me on edge.

Murdered witnesses are common; boat hijacking is ordinary, the tourist crews hacked to death with machetes or shot, the stolen boats used to smuggle loads across the Gulf Stream and then scuttled, boats and bodies disappearing without a trace into the ocean deep. Shark food.

My buddy Callard told me that he was waved away by men with machine guns and guard dogs as he approached the dock at Norman Cay. Later, after asking around, he discovered that the island was owned by a drug runner named Ledher who used the airstrip as a transfer point for cocaine.

Invisible in the darkness, planes land and take off through the night without running lights; the only thing to be seen as they pass by overhead is their hot blue exhaust flame. The thrum of airplane engines flying low overhead is constant. Obviously, the local police are in on the drug trade. It is the country's primary business, and everybody is taking their cut. Obeying the law is a moribund concept.

The next morning I'm up early to visit the submerged plane and dive on it. I return to the channel entrance. The plane in the water is gone. I tack back and forth across the channel and see nothing but clear water and sandy bottom. The plane is simply gone. I steer back from the entrance a quarter-mile and scan down the beach. Behold, there is the plane tipped up on the sand, the cockpit open, obviously stripped.

I am disappointed, but recall that this is how the Bahamians have always made a living—'wracking,'—and they have perfected that skill over two centuries. The whole country makes a beautiful living wracking and smuggling, filling the market gaps left by the merchandise that is illegal on the mainland— drugs now, alcohol during Prohibition. Jack Kennedy's father got rich running Cuban rum to Florida with the help of the Bahamian government, which took its cut in a clever profit sharing arrangement involving guns.

In the quayside cafe, I pass the time with a friendly local. "I see you have a new development under construction. What does it take to get a building permit in this country?"

He laughs into his hand, "Jus' put fifty-thou in an envelope, Mon, and take it to Nassau and hand it to Lynden Pindling."

"So, who the hell is this Lynden Pindling? Is he a building inspector? How does he fit in?"

"He's th' prime minster, Mon."

I'm sailing east when a large powerboat comes up on me and turns parallel alongside, keeping pace two feet from my gunwale. Two dark men stand on deck, and a man is at the wheel above me. They wave and smile and look over my boat with casual interest. Their approach looks suspiciously like a hijacking. I slip my hand beneath a seat cushion and grip the forty-five automatic hidden there. It is loaded and cocked. Fear creeps into my throat. I am a sitting duck. If they invade with pistols, I have no chance. The best I can hope for is to kill the helmsman right above me. If they swing machetes, I can shoot them first. Maybe all three.

I have played out this scenario many times in my imagination. My rule is not to shoot until a person with hostile intent, and without permission, places his foot onto my boat.

With one hand on the butt of the pistol and my other hand on the tiller, I look into their eyes and keep a fraudulent smile beamed directly at them. Shooting the helmsman will be short and fatal; he is less than eight feet from me. In the confusion of that event, I can get off two or three shots at the others before I absorb bullets myself. This could be the end of my tropical island visit and my finish will be quick.

There is no escape. These guys will shoot me at close range, throw my body in the drink and take my boat. A very simple operation from their point of view. The only question in the air: is my boat worth stealing? At hull speed, it can only do six knots, a fast walk. Hardly a vessel to run drugs with. Maybe it's just a robbery. I have some money, some radios, some quickly sold boat equipment; none of it really expensive. But even if it's only a robbery, it will make no difference. It will be bad. The helmsman will die and so will I.

One of the men asks, "Where ya goin', Mon?"

I smile as big as I can, "Nassau? It's over that way ain't it?"

The men turn and point toward the eastern horizon. They nod, "Yas, Mon, it's o' dere."

The powerful boat slowly steers off, opening the narrow gap between us and gently burbles away. The men smile big and wave like departing best friends, "Ave a good sail, Mon," one yells. I smile big and wave back.

At full throttle, the drug runners roar off, their hull slapping the waves like a flat hand on a drumhead until it finally leaps out of sight. As the sound of the powerful boat dissolves into the gentle lap of my bow wave, I release my grip on the pistol and slump back in the cockpit. I look down and watch yellow water drift back and forth between my legs. Cheetos? Is it left over from the Cheetos? I haven't had Cheetos since the Gulf Stream. I absently eye the amber water rippling back and forth. The realization comes slowly—I've pissed my pants.

The rush of fear settles into a black mood. I am not having fun.

THREE BOTTLES

Amidst the glowing coals, fried potato slices in the cast iron skillet float darkly, drowning in grease. All the bacon is gone. The boy is almost too tired to eat after the day of travel: getting the horse off the trailer and loaded with camp gear and food, then hiking five miles with a heavy backpack to this clearing in the aspen grove. His shoulders ache, and his head hurts.

His daddy paid fifty dollars for Joe, the brown horse, so he could carry dead elk out of the mountains. On the hike in, the boy walks behind the horse and watches the drooping bags of food tied on behind the saddle sway and slip a bit with each step. His job is to keep the load from sliding off and falling under the horse's belly. Every two hundred yards the parade stops so the boy can push the bags back up on top.

The horse doesn't seem to care what happens. No matter how hard the boy's cousin hauls on the lead, Joe's pace never changes from his slow dragging walk.

The hunting party set up camp in a small clearing among the fir and aspen trees at ten thousand feet. They had started the hike up to this throw-down camp in the woods at five this morning and had a fire going by sundown. The boy was tired and immediately fell asleep on top of his unrolled sleeping bag, a thin cotton envelope that smelled of age and mold and, in the October nights, offered little warmth and no comfort for his skinny, teenage body.

He was prodded awake with the toe of a hunting boot.

"Eat!" his father orders.

The two men standing by the fire were laughing softly, already drinking whiskey mixed in their coffee before sunrise, their voices muffled by the trees, the short dry weeds around them now trampled flat.

Holding a bottle, the cousin says, "I staked out a game crossing all goddam day between two draws that had several trails going across. Except for those two deer, nuthin' moved. Not a hint of elk. It's too dry. I didn't see a goddam thing move up there all day except those two does that you saw, too."

"Yeah, th' elk aren't movin'," the older man says, "An early snow storm would get th' big bulls movin' down. They spent summer in th' high range. When it cools off, they'll start movin' down." He takes the bottle from the cousin. "When it snows they'll move down."

The boy listens intently. The men know about hunting big game, and he wants to learn about the woods, the outdoors, the animals he will kill. He dreams of killing a big bull elk. In his mind's eye, he can see the target in his sights: big, brown, sporting a big rack four feet across from tip to tip. He can see the elk flinch and then collapse when the bullet hits him in the neck and breaks his spine.

By the third night, the hunters are tired and discouraged. They see no game. They are running short of food. The plan was to kill an elk and cook its heart and liver with some potatoes and fried apples. But there is no elk meat.

The cousin tosses an empty whiskey bottle onto the trash pile and says, "There's nother dead sojer. We need summor." The boy laughs at his cousin's joke.

The father says, "We'll send the kid down to the pickup in the morning. We need grub, too. We're outta eggs and almost bacon. He can pick up some more grub, and some gas for the lantern. He ain't doin' nuthin'."

"What about the booze?" the cousin says, "We're outta booze. There's three bottles a whiskey left behind the seat of my pickup. He can bring them bottles back, too."

"Yeah. That's what we need worst of all," the father says.

"Yeah," the cousin says, "Hey Kid, yur the gofer. Gopher the booze. I'm gettin' kinda dried out up here." They all laugh.

The boy shivers through the night. The thin sleeping bag laid atop a canvas tarp yields no comfort; whatever touches the ground turns cold and stays cold. He often dreams of his father towering above him, slapping him. He tastes the blood in his mouth.

Dawn is a relief. He stands with the two men close to the morning fire which spits and flares, warming those spots that never warmed during the miserable night. At sunrise, the light slants through the tree limbs and traces a random pattern on the dry earth.

"Here," the cousin says with a lopsided smile, handing the boy a bottle of Mogen David wine, "Have a drink. It'll make your pecker hard."

The schoolboy tips the bottle back and swallows. He has never tasted liquor. It is good, like edgy grape juice. But better.

"OOOOKay," the cousin says capping the bottle, "When you go down to the pickup, don ferget to get the three bottles b'hind the seat. That's what we need the most!"

"I'll do it," the boy says softly. "I really like that wine. Can I have another slug?"

"No. The next thing you'll be a wino down on skid row. What'll yore daddy think of that?"

"Well, I don' think he'd care one way or th' other."

The cousin smiles.

As he rides downhill toward the truck, the sun warms the boy enough for him to shed his jacket and stuff it into his backpack with the canteen of water. Old Joe is a joy to ride; he never breaks his plodding pace and that suits the boy fine since he has never ridden a horse. Joe doesn't make fast moves or even look back. A perfect horse. The army surplus saddle, bought for ten dollars, is hard and he squirms, trying to find a place for his boney buttocks to get comfortable. Nothing works.

At the dust-coated pickup, he ties Joe's reins to the bumper, removes food from boxes and drops it into canvas bags, then fishes around behind the seat of the pickup. The three bottles of whiskey lay in a row. He stands them up side-by-side in the tote-bag.

He discovers some stale sweet rolls in a brown, oil-stained bag, sits on the tailgate and relishes one at a time, chewing slowly, savoring the sweetness. He looks around at the mountains beyond the camp, focusing on the sloping land between here and the camp, and tries to pick out the draws and drainages he crossed on the way down. The low places blend into the slopes and aspen groves; the rising ground looks flat, but he knows this is deceptive. I'm glad there is a clear trail to follow back to camp, he thinks. I'd hate to get lost up here.

Joe swishes his tail at the black flies that hum around him. They land and bite and he shivers his skin to shoo them off.

The city boy has never looked closely at a horse. He studies Joe carefully...big head, the boy thinks, all bone...ears that twitch. Muscles in the front curve down to skinny legs. Why are they built like that, big body on these skinny legs? Big feet...too big for the legs...and the ass end...muscular...big thigh muscles...again on skinny legs. Makes no sense. When his eyes are half closed, Joe doesn't look too smart. Well, this dumb horse is going to take me back to camp. That's all I ask. It was a good ride down to the pickup. I like Joe. Joe is slow; I'm happy for that; no quick moves.

The boy lays in the warm pickup bed for a while and thinks about hunting and killing. I like animals. Why kill them? he thinks.

The old war surplus rifle that was loaned to him uses off-size hand-loaded bullets. When he was sighting the rifle in, one of the bullets didn't fire at all and he ejected it out on the ground and there it lay, shiny and dangerous; he kicked dirt over it. The next three rounds fired.

In time, he falls asleep, images of the old man swinging at him, slapping him, floating through the midday dream. After an hour he wakes as the sun shines hotly on him and his face begins to burn. His brain is sleep-fuzzy. I hate him when he slaps me around, he thinks, but all kids get slapped around, I guess.

He loads Joe with the lumpy sacks of food and works to balance the load, so it doesn't slip around.

It's early afternoon, and the sun slides lower, and the shadows stretch longer, but there is still plenty of time to get back to camp before sundown. As slow as Joe walks it'll take a couple of hours.

They hit the well-used game trail. Joe plods along; his shoes occasionally kicks a rock that gives a metallic ring. Otherwise, he steps quietly, leaving tiny puffs of dust. This is a dry October. It hasn't rained in weeks.

Joe seems to know where they are going and the boy lets Joe have his head. Occasionally the horse snatches up a bunch of dry grass alongside the trail.

"Good boy, Joe," the rider says and pats the horse's neck.

He looks to the West. A shelf of dark clouds billows over the gray peaks. They look wet, he thinks. The land and the trees and the animals will love some moisture, and it may push the big game down to where we can kill some.

I don't want to get caught out here, though. The rain will be cold because it always is, but I will be beside the campfire before it hits.

The gentle motion of the horse, and the sun, warming the boy, causes him to nod. Then, with a start, he comes fully awake. Suddenly, the trail is smaller, fainter and nearly level. He stands in the stirrups and tries to see what is ahead. They are in a shallow canyon. Ahead he sees the canyon getting deeper and darker and the trail narrower, less distinct. His suspicion grows slowly. On the way down we were never in a canyon. Joe must have taken the wrong path. We should be going up, not down.

"Damn it, Joe, where didja turn off?"

Again, he stops to adjust the sacks of food, lifting them back into position behind the saddle. Staring at the saddle, he can't figure out how to re-tie it so that the load stays put.

The canyon falls into full shadow. The boy stands beside an aspen tree and tries to think. I'm in this canyon, and I should be up there, a couple of hundred feet higher, up top, up on the flat, on the real trail and turning uphill toward camp. But first, we have to get out of this canyon. If we backtrack on this trail, it is at least a mile to the real trail. But if we climb out of the canyon straight up the side we should intersect the main trail on top without backtracking a foot. It'll be tough because the canyon wall is steep and covered with bunch grass and trees but the footing looks okay.

He grabs Joe's reins and begins to lead him uphill. The mount doesn't want to go that way and keeps swinging his head as if saying no. Pulling the reins over his shoulder, the boy begins to climb one steep step at a time. Joe follows but keeps tossing his head and pulling back. In the quiet wilderness, the only sounds are Joe's breaths, the creaking saddle, the boy's puffing. Out of sight, crows caw, the calls bouncing around the canyon. Occasionally the whiskey bottles clink together. He stops and takes one of the whiskey bottles out of the canvas bag, puts a couple of apples between the two left, wraps his jacket around the lone bottle and puts the bundle in his backpack.

He pulls the horse. In especially steep spots he reaches up with his free hand and grabs a knob of bunchgrass to pull them up.

Colder air begins to sneak down the canyons from the high country. Now, the gray clouds roll overhead and the late afternoon sunlight pinches out. A cool breeze with a hint of cold hits his face. The boy stretches the reins taught.

"Now, dang it, Joe, this is the only way outta here so quit fightin' me."

Joe's ears flatten, and he closes his eyes. The steep climb and pulling Joe are tiring; the boy's legs burn and his shoulder aches where the reins cut across.

He sits down and leans back against the steep wall. Joe blows hard.

Fear rises in his throat. "Damn you, Joe, if ya don't help, we are never gonna get outta here. You are one worthless horse."

After a couple of minutes, he stands and starts pulling again; they come out to a flatter place in the canyon side. He mounts Joe and kicks him to go.

Joe moves a few steps then, without warning, steps off the trail and downhill towards a big aspen tree. A thick branch hits the boy in the chest, and he feels himself falling backward over the horse's rump. He hits the ground and feels a sharp pain in his ribs. The food sack falls on top of him. Lying still, he waits for the first flash of pain to fade. Then he smells whiskey.

On the ground, he rolls over and slips his shoulders out of the backpack. He lays in the dry leaves and tries to catch his breath. It slowly comes back. His ribs hurt. The whiskey smell is strong. He unbuckles the flap of the pack. Amber liquid drains out onto the weeds. Broken glass, wet with liquor, is scattered everywhere inside the backpack.

The tree limbs above form a lacy pattern against the scudding clouds. He feels a wet snowflake melt on his face. He struggles to stand; he stretches his hand against the hillside to steady himself until the dizziness passes. He shakes out the jacket. It is soaked. After a minute or two he pulls on the stinking coat.

"Damn you, Joe; ya did that on purpose. I outta shoot ya, ya mean sombitch! You are going to get us hurt."

Fear replaces the pain, it rises in his throat, then tears come and smear his vision. He screams, "If I had fifty bucks to pay for ya I'd shoot ya and leave ya here for the danged buzzards!" Joe stands off, ears erect. He chews quietly.

By the time the boy has reassembled the freight and got it back atop Joe's back, the shadows are gone and the last exhausting climb out of the canyon brings them out on top of the vaguely familiar slope. The fading light makes shades of black and gray.

Near full dark, the boy looks hard and finds the trace of a trail and turns uphill toward where he hopes the camp in the trees is located. Sweat from the climb cools and his body, fully drained, chills. His ribs give sharp pains.

"I just hope I can find the camp. It's dangerous out here," he says aloud. It is getting wetter and colder. He shivers and kicks Joe hard, the horse's ears flatten but Joe doesn't change his lazy pace.

My old man will be pissed off that I'm late. Way late. I should have been back before sundown. He is going to beat on me, I just know it. He always does when I don't do exactly what he says.

While dozing on his sleeping bag, he'd heard his father mumble to the cousin, "That boy's the camp nigger...not worth much...not worth anything...useless..."

"Joe, ya gonna make us spend all night out here. I know what is going to happen. The old man is gonna be pissed and beat the hell outta me if we don't get back. He might anyway because of the whiskey."

"It'll be bad," he says. "I'm gonna get my ass kicked because of you, ya sombitch! You're a sorry excuse for a huntin' horse ya sombitch."

Joe slowly walks on, his wet head hanging down.

It is dark. The trail is hard to see and looks much narrower and dimmer than it did in daylight. Side trails take off here and there. The boy questions himself: Am I on the right path? Am I lost? This is scary. Maybe somewhere back there I missed the main trail. God, I don't want to be lost. Maybe they will never find me. I hate this. I can freeze to death out here. I can die.

He is cold all over except where his legs touch Joe's belly. The big flakes of falling snow make everything look wet and fuzzy. In the darkness, he can see the silhouettes of the treetops, but that is all. The groves are blots of blurred blackness.

Out of the depths of the trees, suddenly, there's a tiny yellow flicker. As they turn toward the amber spot, it becomes a campfire, snapping from the wet wood. The men talk across the fire; their voices carry through the trees. Relief flows over the boy.

He holds his ribs and slowly dismounts a few yards away throwing the reins over a deadfall.

"Where the hell have you been?" the father yells. "You were supposed to be back hours ago, boy. Ya been screwing the dog, as usual, haven't cha?"

"I'm sorry, sir."

The man walks over to him and slaps the boy hard on the side of his head, then stops the boy's fall with a slap from the other hand. The boy's ears ring.

"Unload that horse!" the father barks.

Silently crying, the boy unties and throws down the food sacks into the wet snow.

Shouldering the boy out of the way, the cousin snatches up a canvas bag, "This is the important part!" he says, and pulls two bottles out and sets them on the ground.

He says, "Damn, you stink, boy! Didja get in ta the whiskey? I thought there were three. Where's th' other one?"

"One of 'em broke."

"How th' hell did you break it? How th' hell did that happen?"

"I don't know. The horse jus' took off. It wasn't my fault."

His father steps up and slaps him hard. "You are worthless!" he spits, then turns and walks back to the fire.

The boy stares angrily at the ground. I hate hunting. I hate being called the camp nigger. I hate the horse. I hate my old man. I hate my cousin. I hate everything.

He walks over to his bedroll and picks up his hunting rifle, a battlefield trophy lifted from the stinking body of a Japanese soldier on Peleliu. He throws the bolt and chambers a bullet. His trembling shakes the rifle. He raises it and tries to hold it steady. Tears smear the sight picture; his pulse beats in his ears. His finger feels the serrations on the trigger; slowly he squeezes. His father's face is encircled in the iron sight, his angry face looms large, his eyes red, his fists swinging.

Aiming at Joe's skull, the boy pulls the trigger, the gun snaps. Joe continues chewing oats. The boy can see the animal crashing to the forest floor with a hollow grunt, his hooves thrashing last, reflexive, running steps that leave semi-circular scrapes in the sodden brown leaves.

But the bullet doesn't fire.

"Whadda ya think you're doin', boy?" his dad yells.

"Nuthin'," the boy says.

FLEA BAILEY'S GIRL

I'm looking for a place to take shelter. The wind is up and my radio antenna at the masthead is flailing around loose and needs to be reattached before the wires get fatigued and break off.

Sailing by Great Harbour Cay, I spot a sharply defined cut deep into a rocky cliff that leads inside the island, its sheer walls on each side at least as tall as my mast. Slowly, carefully, I ease my boat through the cut into the lagoon and up to an empty dock.

There is nobody around and I tie up opposite a luxury motor yacht.

I dig out my Jumars—line ascenders used by mountaineers that latch onto a vertical rope and allow one to climb it. This mountaineering device, attached to a rope, easily slides up, then locks onto the line. By placing my feet in the attached slings, I step, lock, and walk up the halyard to the masthead.

As I hang at the top of the mast, thirty feet above the deck, the lightweight boat lists over twenty-five degrees, thus I work over my head. I work to fit the antenna base back into its socket. My hands shake a bit. Heights scare me. And I've never had to trust Jumars before. Hanging upside down, I look around and down at the white yacht next door. A crewman comes out on deck and waves to me. I wave back.

He laughs up at me, "That's a helluva trick."

"Yeah. One of my mountain climbing buddies taught me that."

"Are you a mountain climber?"

"Are you kidding? I have acrophobia so bad that I have been known to throw up, so if I were you, I would be sure to stand a bit more upwind."

The man moves.

Down on the dock, he introduces himself. "My name is Bill; I am the skipper of this boat for Flea Bailey."

"Flee who?"

"You know, the famous lawyer, F. Lee Bailey. He defended Patty Hearst. He's famous."

"Oh, that Flea Bailey."

"Are you alone?"

"Yep."

"Single handing?"

"Yep."

"You crossed the Gulf Stream in that Clorox bottle?"

"Yep."

There is a long quiet while he eyeballs my boat, "You got bigger balls than me then. We crossed it with a crew of three in a fifty-four-footer and I was worried a couple of times."

"Well, thanks. It doesn't take balls; it takes boundless ignorance."

He laughs. "You wanna join us for dinner? Flea is buying for the crew. You can come along." He points toward the beach. "There's a decent restaurant right over there."

The sky is red at sundown, and I relax in the cockpit, watching the action around the harbor and the people drinking under the trees. Flea's crew steps onto the dock and Bill says, "You comin'?"

In the comfortable room heavily accented with wood and paper placemats, the men pick a table for six. Four of us seat ourselves;

I randomly single out a chair between empty seats and listen to the crew talk about maintenance chores they have yet to do. Then, this short, stocky man with a large head arrives with a woman.

I stand and put out my hand. "I'm Jerry."

"Lee," he says perfunctorily and drops my hand. I turn to his companion and she says, "I'm Cath," with a heart-stopping smile. My reality dissolves. She is the most beautiful woman I have ever seen. She sits. I can't take my eyes off her. I can feel my heart thump in my chest.

With Flea to my left and his woman to my right, I am totally indifferent to him. He could have been John Wayne or the President of the United States. I turn my back to him, a dominant male move. Any minute I expect him to tap me on the shoulder as a warning to leave his woman alone.

Cath's vibe is mesmerizing, sexual; her noble face is framed by auburn hair that shines, her lips are full and sensuous; her gray eyes spellbinding. This is a woman of men's wet dreams. I think, God almighty, save me from what I'm thinking. I would seriously consider murder to have her. I've got nothing to lose; just imagine kissing her, fondling her, loving her, being alone with all this astounding beauty until dark. Ah, darkness. I contemplate an amorous night with this woman and silently sigh.

The famous lawyer looks into his plate, bored, preoccupied, lost in thought. He ignores us all. He says nothing to me or anyone else. I forget about him being at the table.

I lose all consciousness of the conversation that I'm having with Cath; I haven't seen a woman this lovely in years, maybe ever. Everything real disappears. When she looks at me, there is no other reality, no other world. Just us.

She is smart, educated, poised, polite, a perfect example of idealized womanhood. I am instantly in love with every graceful move of her hands, the curl of her fingers, every soft word, every sweet breath. Her eyes hold me immobile. I listen with my whole soul. I decide that if, by some heavenly miracle, she asks me to fly off with her, I will get up from the table, tell Flea Bailey, "Tough shit, Buddy," leave my boat and ratty clothes, and walk away with her without a plan or a dollar for tomorrow. Just sleeping with her once would satisfy me for life. For me, Flea doesn't exist.

I think about her for days. The memory of our hour's conversation is reduced to a feeling. I realize I can't remember a single thing we said to each other—only her eyes and the fantasy of touching her face, her neck, her breast. I envy Flea beyond the rational. What does that short little shit have that I don't besides wealth and fame and a fifty-four-foot boat and a crew of three and the most incredible woman I have ever seen in my life?

Now me? I could give her adoration and respect and good conversation. I might be able to make her laugh again, that tinkling, genuine, warm and honest laugh that thrilled me in my gut. When dinner was finished and she stood and left the table, walking away with that short little guy, I felt a loss, a hollowness like a small death, knowing I would never see her again.

In my bunk I fantasize. With people like her on the earth, I realize that being alive is good and life is worth living. I also realize how lonely I am, how alone and detached from reality I have been. This woman made me feel like a man again, ready to attack whatever is to come, new adventures, new horizons. Lying in my berth, I think about her, and even though she is a fantasy, I soak in her fantasy like a warm bath.

But, I'm on a sailboat in the Bahamas; living the dream of men who work in big city offices with views of brick walls and kids and a wife at home in the burbs. I should feel good about being here, about my accomplishments, about surviving. I should but I don't. Attention Deficit Disorder has kicked in. I'm actually bored.

Sweet Jesus, what is happening to me? I have to find a woman. I can't stand myself anymore. I hate being alone.

GET FIRED

The weather is perfect at The Marriott Hotel in Palm Springs. The encompassing luxury and rarified air smells expensive, if not intoxicating.

One of the largest computer services firm in the world is having a meeting of senior managers here, so the place is crawling with intelligent men in ten-dollar haircuts and white shirts. The men's clothes do not match their importance. These are technical experts for chrissake, afloat in a haughtier-than-thou attitude, and this meeting place is extremely high end.

Iris, my partner in our executive sales training business, and I, have taught persuasion to some of these executives for years. While some people believe that selling is duplicitous by its very nature, we teach that the buyer is not a 'mark.' We teach that the seller ascertains the personal goals of the buyer and then helps them get there. Engagement with the client, from our perspective, is not about you; it's about them. That's how trust is built, the single most important factor in long-term consulting relationships.

The keynote speaker is the crowd pleaser of this meeting. The big guy preaches to an SRO crowd for forty-five minutes about the glories of the firm, the big money the stockholders are making, and the brilliant future that stretches to eternity or the Second Coming, whichever comes first. There is spotty, interrupting applause and, occasionally, spontaneous outbursts of yelled enthusiasm for the bonuses.

To my great disappointment, the clients who furnish the money and lifestyle for these people are not mentioned even by implication; there is not a peep about concern for their clients' business health, well-being, or their survival in a dog-eat-dog world, nor a token nod towards gratitude for what their clients do for them daily, i.e., furnish the money for their heady lifestyle. The keynote speech is all about the 'organizational me' and 'how very good we are' and 'how we are the smartest consultants in the field and the money we make supports our executives' heavily compensated retirement income and golden parachutes.'

As the sales training firm hired by the senior executives, Iris and I have worked for years teaching a client-consciousness that moves these consultants away from the self-importance and self-dealing that is systemic in the consulting business. We teach that if the clients are well-served, the firm and its people also will fare well, that it is a symbiotic relationship, not a zero-sum game where we win, they lose. It has proven over time to be the most successful approach; the consultant's success is always a bounce shot off the wall of the client's success.

The early evening gathering at the edge of the endless swimming pool seems the picture of California desert glamour. Champagne flows, crab-legs are splayed, inviting gustatory rape, and a subtle quartet alternately plays classical or Sinatra. Standing around like an outsider, I watch these professionals do what they do best—opine—boasting about being better than the great unwashed, smarter than the competitors, gullible, and computer ignorant clients.

Eavesdropping outside a circle of men I hear, "How much money did we take off that client?" Snicker…snicker…

Chuckling, another smug professional chimes in, "A lot."

While anger is part of my makeup I generally keep it under control in professional situations, however, these guys and their arrogance suddenly broke my thermometer; anger boiled up to my ears and higher.

We had spent years training these highly educated people to speak in their clients' language, to be concerned about their clients' well-being, that there were human considerations beyond just the money. We had proven over and over again that the largest gains came from empathizing with the client in both thought and deed.

Right there by the crab-legs and coconut cookies I suddenly realized that all our efforts had fallen on deaf ears, that these executives were willing to pay any financial price to appear as though they cared, when, in fact, their only concerns were their own personal power and income.

Seething, I left the champagne bubbles and casual bullshit and made my way back to our luxurious room. I flicked the news on for a while, hoping to calm down but ultimately opted for bed. With Iris.

Gritting my teeth, I say, "Iris, I think I am going crazy."

"I understand," she says softly.

And I know she does. We have been a team in life and work for two decades. She is my exquisite lover and full business partner. She is smarter than me and a better teacher. She is beautiful both outside and inside, a southern girl who spends a goodly part of her time running downfield blocking for me because, if you want something badly screwed up, I'm your man.

We would never have been this good if it had been left to me. I wrote our material over a period of fifteen years but Iris has always been the brains behind our success. We reached the apex of our craft because of her attention to detail and observations about life. She is the best salesperson I've ever watched work.

She outthinks the competition and takes assignments away from the most famous competitors in the business.

So, even though I know I'm off the rails I'm in good hands. Sleep, however, does not come. I toss and turn and pound the pillow the whole night, the clients' offensive comments playing and obsessively replaying throughout the night.

"How much money did we take off that client?" Laughter...

The question and laugh cycled and recycled. It just wouldn't let go.

"Sleep!" I commanded myself. "Go to sleep!"

"How much money...," Laugh...

On and on until dawn when I get up, shower and dress. My head hurts. This very morning I have a one-hour gig with a room full of executives reviewing the central theme of building trust with your client. Can I control my anger? Of course, I am a professional. And this isn't my firm. These people don't work for me; I work for them in short intensive bursts. My income doesn't rely on theirs. My income doesn't rely on their reputation. Can I keep my cool? Of course, I have been standing in front of executives for two decades. I know what I am doing. I am a pro.

Standing in front of the room full of attentive faces I am insanely angry; I try to still my internal voice.

I start with, "Good morning. As you know, my name is Jerry Vass, I am a professional salesman and a professional sales trainer. It's good to see you all again. You know I have been working with your senior dealmakers for years but yesterday I heard something that seriously put me off my feed."

I pause and take a deep breath. The anger roars back.

"Yesterday afternoon I was standing by a group of men on the lawn and overheard a senior guy ask, 'How much money did we take off that client?' Then he laughed."

A few men grin. They stare at me.

A cloud of anger descends over my eyes. "Just who do you people think you are? After all the money you've spent, all the education and training you've had, you still believe that the customer is simply a mark for your avarice and you are perfectly comfortable saying out loud that you are only in this job for the money?"

I start shaking with rage and over the next half-hour, escalate into a real, military-style ass-chewing. Then I lob my final grenade: "You say you are in the service business, but you are not! You are in the self-service business. As highly educated professionals, you should all be utterly ashamed of yourselves!"

A break is called and I am invited out into the hallway by the senior executive who fires me on the spot.

My hubris and temper cost Iris, the finest executive sales trainer in America, at least $200,000 in training services. To her (and only her) I confessed that I had been a completely insufferable asshole.

HARBOR POLICE

Business requires me to return briefly to the mainland.

I leave my boat anchored in a protected little backwater in Spanish Wells because, unlike the rest of the islands, the people here are honest. One can tell by seeing the line of small boats tied up along the shore, their outboard motors still hanging temptingly off their transoms. In a dishonest society, on other islands, they would have been long gone.

The telephone call from my boat-watcher is not good news. My boat has been broken into and equipment is missing. The news depresses me. In the past few weeks fooling around on the boat has been boring. I liked it while I was learning how to survive but now I dread living in tight quarters. Being owned by a floating object that is a money sponge is wearing on me.

Flying back to the island, I climb aboard my sailboat and discover that all of the emergency equipment is missing: the radios, the emergency locator beacon, flare gun, even the reefing jib I had sewn specially for this boat and this trip.

The boat-watcher says disgustedly, "There were some loudmouths anchored close by, and they yelled back and forth all the time...totally obnoxious. On the day they left, I heard one of them yell they were sailing to Nassau.

Riding the mail-boat to Nassau, I closely consider what course of action I will take. Can I find the thieves? There are lots of boats out here and lots of places to go. But they had a low, homemade plywood boat, about a twenty-four-footer, according to my man, so that's a start.

One of my missing items is a cockpit awning, a canvas shade that blocks out the hot sun while anchored. I stand at the railing of the mail-boat as it eases by the anchored vessels lining the harbor. There is not a hoisted sail or canvas among them; nothing to be seen but bare poles, except for one little white vessel with a cockpit cover shading it. As we pass close by, I can see two people with drinks in their hands in the shade of an awning supported by a halyard.

"That's their boat," my man whispers, "those are the totally obnoxious assholes."

So, what do I do now? I might go to the beach, buy a baseball bat, have a water-taxi take me out there, step aboard their boat, beat the hell out of the guy, break some bones and take my stuff back. I can do that.

But what if he has a gun? Everybody carries a gun out here. He has every right to shoot me if he has the same rules I have—step aboard the boat uninvited and it is open season on attackers. Maybe attacking the guy is not a good idea.

The mail-boat docks near the town. I find a Bahamian policeman on a street corner, who directs me to his lieutenant. The lieutenant is a dark Bahamian, serious, unsmiling. Dressed in a two-piece blue suit, white shirt and an awful tie with a big knot, he is heavy set, shorter than me but obviously strong and fit. I tell him my story of the theft from my boat in Spanish Wells and about the thieves drinking on their small boat anchored close.

"In an hour, meet me at the police dock, and we go find out," he says.

I step onto the police launch. There is nothing subtle about the motor boat. It is forty feet of black hull with white three-foot lettering that loudly announces 'HARBOR POLICE,' a sign that can be easily read from three hundred yards. Its diesel engine barks to life and the exhaust gurgles authoritatively, the bass engine sounds bounce off the dock buildings. I stand in the back of the launch with the lieutenant and point toward the sailboat target.

As we idle up the channel, heads pop up out of anchored, silent boats. Their crews hear the authoritative engine and watch the threatening black vessel with red spotlights and a siren on top glide by announcing its intimidating presence.

As we rumble along, I remember an unmistakable feature of the cockpit cover I had bought from my sailing buddy. His name was neatly stenciled on the hem.

I borrow a pencil from the officer and write my buddy's name inside a matchbook cover and hand to him, "This name is on the canvas," I say.

He takes it, reads it, nods, and slips it into his suit-coat pocket.

Approaching the suspect vessel, we look down into its cockpit. We ease alongside the much smaller boat and the edge of the canvas floats into view exactly at eye level. The stenciled name on the canvas cover slides in front of the officer's eyes: "Callard." I couldn't have planned it more cinematically. I stifle a laugh.

The officer glances at me with a knowing nod.

Bending low under the canvas he then orders the man, "Standby to take our line."

The thin man, wearing shorts and a dirty wife-beater, looks alarmed, "What's this about?"

The officer answers evenly, sounding almost friendly, "You have stolen property that belongs to this man." He thumbs over his shoulder.

"Oh, my God, certainly not! I own everything on this boat."

The officer holds the edge of the canvas between his blunt fingers, "Where did you get this cover?"

"I found it on float," Undershirt says firmly.

I pull the edge of the canvas onto my tongue and taste it. It tastes sweet. I turn to the officer, "This canvas has never been in saltwater."

The cop's attitude instantly turns hard and threatening. Suddenly, he looks angry, bigger, meaner, a representative of the law.

He turns to me and orders, "Go aboard. Start up at the front of the boat and work your way back. Go through everything and pass me back your property."

I crawl inside the low cabin and into the bow. At the front of the v-berth, in plain sight, is my jib in a sail bag. I hand the orange bag back to the officer who is now stooping inside the low cabin. My emergency locator beacon is next. I pass that back to him. And then two radios.

I am angry. This worthless piece of shit stole my survival gear. He didn't care about my life, and I sure-as-hell don't care about his. He can go to jail for years as far as I'm concerned.

Looking back at Undershirt, who sits in the cockpit beside a woman, the policeman asks, "Where you from?"

"Calgary," the man answers sullenly, looking at the deck.

Tucked underneath a mattress, I feel the plastic case of my flare gun. I bought it because if I was going to die at sea, I wanted everybody within miles to know about it; to light up the sky with fireworks as my last sinking act. I hand the case back to the cop.

"That's my flare gun," Undershirt declares, his voice cracking.

"No, it isn't," I say. "When you buy a new flare gun, they come with three flares. I bought extras." I say to the officer. "If you open the case, it will have six extra flares. There are eight rounds in the case and one loaded in the pistol chamber. And that pistol is loaded, by the way." I say.

The officer opens the case and, pointing at each, counts the flares aloud. He stops at eight.

He then removes the blunt-barreled flare gun from the case, looks at it carefully, rotating his hand, fits his finger to the trigger and pulls. With a loud pop, the ninth pyrotechnic projectile shoots two feet down into a pile of clothes, spewing red hot flame at two thousand degrees; it hisses wildly, shooting high-pressure fire into the pile of dirty clothes which instantly blazes.

Fire!

Hot fear seizes me.

I hold my breath and anticipate the exploding gasoline fumes that are lying low, trapped in the bilge just waiting for a spark. Fearing the flash, I dive onto the stack of flaming clothes and the flame-spewing flare, seize it all bare handed, and throw the whole fireball over the side. The dangerous hot mess, now hissing two-foot flames, drifts away.

From the anchored sail boats nearby, yachtie heads pop out all around us. Fire burning on the water? A hot red pyrotechnic spouting flame? All from a small sailboat with the Harbor Patrol tied to it? What the hell is going on? Twenty feet from the boat, the flare spits and drowns. Smoke lazes out low across the water's surface.

The Lieutenant, Undershirt, and I begin the trip back to the police dock; Undershirt sits on the fantail railing scowling at the deck.

I step over to him, "You know, if you give me the money for the stuff that you sold to other boaters, I won't press charges."

He looks angry. He shakes his head, "I don't have any money."

"Well, man, I suggest that we make a deal. You don't wanna go to jail in the Bahamas. You're a white man, and the jailers are black, know whut I mean?"

The lieutenant steps between us, "Don't talk to the prisoner," he barks.

We all obey his command. Motoring back to the dock, nobody talks. I watch Undershirt. He is a man under high stress. Sweat dribbles down from his armpits and occasionally, looking at the deck, he shakes his head.

The next morning, I go the courthouse to recover my stolen goods. The clerk inventories it and I sign the paper that says I received it. I look out the tall window in the courtroom and see a black man being urged along by a Bahamian policeman holding a shotgun muzzle to the back of the prisoner's skull.

Around mid-morning, Undershirt enters the courtroom in handcuffs and, steered by the guard, sits on the front bench beneath the judge's eyes.

I lean over from behind and whisper, "How's jail?"

He blanches, "It's unbelievable, it's a hellhole."

"So what're ya gonna do now?"

"I don't know," he whispers. "They say I'm gonna go to jail for two years...I know I won't live two years in that place...they'll kill me. Another prisoner told me that I could bribe my way outta this for $5000...my girlfriend is on her way back to Calgary to raise the money." He takes a deep breath. "I just hope I can stay alive until she gets back."

The bailiff, a giant of a black man in uniform, walks over. "No talking to the prisoner," he hisses.

Suddenly I find myself feeling sorry for the guy with the skinny arms poking out of a dirty undershirt. "Good luck," I say to the back of his head.

The guard towers over me and glares, "I say no talkin', Mon. You wanna go to jail, too?"

Returning to my anchored vessel, I throw my equipment back into the cabin, snap a new lock to the hatch-cover and go ashore. I look back at my pretty little craft. She has given me pleasure and many adventurous miles but I find myself thinking, "This is the end for us, Honey. I'll have someone come and get you."

The opposite of love is indifference. About Street Hustler, I feel indifferent.

It's time to give up this silliness, I think, to travel on to a new place, see new things, meet new people, think new thoughts. Maybe take Iris with me; she throws a fire blanket over my insanity, keeps me out of trouble. Mostly.

VIET NAM

The thunderstorms over DC cancelled my flight so I was left with walking around gawking at the marble monuments.

If Abe Lincoln shifts his stony and benevolent gaze just a bit to the left from the Reflecting Pool and the Washington Monument, he can peer through the elm trees down into the negative space of the Viet Nam War Memorial.

It is negative space because it sits in the ground beneath eye level, a grave hole commemorating the dead, where black marble slabs march solemnly in rank to an unheard dirge down into an ever-deepening V in the earth.

The black, polished surfaces, incised with sharply cut, sandblasted names, reflect colorful images of the visitors ghosting silently by.

An unspoken agreement hangs in the air—visitors understand that this is a hallowed place. Voices are hushed. Offerings to the memories of lost sons and husbands and fathers and daughters are laid along the bottom of the standing granite slabs. Bright blossoms are strewn about on the worn grass or stand singly in pots. White wreaths hang on black Styrofoam crosses. And other more intimate articles are there as well: among the blossoms lie a well-used camouflaged cover for a helmet and an olive-drab fatigue hat with the bright label "Airborne" stitched on the top.

The slabs are numbered so you can locate the names of the lost. Soft searching fingers tentatively trace out the sculpted names of the remembered. Faces fall in sadness when the searchers find and touch the ghost names. Memories and stone letters blur and flow together in quiet tears.

A large man in full fatigues, black beret and slickly polished jump boots hunts carefully up and down the memorial looking for the names of his friends, when he does, his fingers gently and lovingly caress them.

Jetliners from National Airport roar overhead shutting out the possibility of conversation behind a wall of sound. A helicopter wop-wops over and the parachutist looks into the sky, listening to the rush and beat of rotors. His eyes look tired. He looks old. Today he re-lives yesterday. The line of pilgrims separates and flows around him like water around a rock.

The reflections move along, colorful and diffused, a Monet impression of today's living things seen from the hard, dark side of combat. Somewhere, a sprinkler head arcs staccato water across the greensward.

The air is stifling. The sound of children flows out of the trees; a half dozen little girls run through a sprinkler, the water soaking their shoes. Their delighted squeals rise and fall, heard even over the jet noise. A park ranger sprints across the lawn waving his arms and frightens them off, "You girls go away, no screaming here," he commands.

People with cameras jockey for position along the wall. Mother waits patiently for Father to click a remembrance to take home—a two-dimensional image of a three-dimensional son removed by explosive fortune to some fourth dimension.

A slim jogger, wearing only shorts, trots up to the wall. He perspires heavily. He stops and hovers over a directory of names held in a thick, brass glass-covered stand. Bending over this book of the dead his finger shakes and traces down the column of names. He turns a page. Then another. Slowly, his finger travels down the list, then it stops. For many moments he is still.

Drops of sweat fall and splatter onto the glass top. With a quick, nervous swipe of his hand, he smears the drops of moisture off the glass. Or were they tears?

HEARING BURMA

Iris and I are staying in a second-class hotel in Yangon, nee-Rangoon, Myanmar, nee-Burma. It is hot and humid, just a step away from the Equator, and my hearing aid has broken. The 'in-ear' piece of the device is connected to the 'behind-the-ear' piece with an almost invisible tube through which flows a wire called the 'connectatuda.' The tube looks like a mouse's intestine, it is very tiny and transparent and now, broken.

Which leaves me with the unsettling possibility of spending two weeks on a river boat without hearing conversations about exciting new recipes, women's fashion, how to prepare food in this new democracy and what's on deck for tomorrow's activities.

A frightening prospect.

What is the first step to finding a repairman who works on digital Costco hearing aids? Here?

I go directly to the hotel Concierge and show him the problem, setting into play a series of hotly argued conferences involving the registration clerk, security guard, business coordinator, doorman, taxi hailer, luggage walla, and lobby dust-mopper. Together they come up with the Oriental concept that—nobody knows nothing.

But...after referencing the Internet, the Yellow Pages and a half-dozen phone calls, the smiling Concierge says he might have a solution and asks me earnestly, "Can you spend one thousand 300 kyet?"

"How much is that in dollars?"

"Is about six dollars," he says apologetically.

"Yes, I think I can manage that," I say, also earnestly.

"Go here first." He Xs a map with a ball point pen. "These people say they have."

I tip him ten bucks.

Jumping into a taxi, Iris and I find the audio equipment specialist in a tiny office in downtown Rangoon. That expert works hard to sell me a new $1400 hearing aid somewhat like my broken one.

Holding my fractured instrument in the air, he says, "So sorry; no parts of this one. We carry different," he says apologetically.

Onward with Plan B—a visit to the best pharmacy in the largest city in Burma. Maybe, but only maybe, they have over-the-counter hearing aids. I've never heard of such things, but it's worth a try; the Concierge says so.

In the pharmacy, a storefront on a side street chock-a-block with every kind of DIY health appliance designed to improve teeth, eyes, ears, kidneys, weight, bowels, sex, and normal wellbeing, we enter our personal world of hearing Nirvana. The store is stacked with cardboard boxes reaching halfway to the ceiling.

I tap my ear with a forefinger.

"Yes, we got," says the serious clerk. She places three different devices on the counter priced from six dollars all the way up to a luxury high of eight dollars. "You like test?" she says in a voice that is more of a command than a request.

Out of an abundance of both doubt and caution, I put the six-dollar model in my ear. I can hear, perhaps better than my computer-tuned, behind the ear, nearly invisible hearing aids designed and built in Sweden with a transparent, "can't see'em" intestine that is about the price of a used Toyota.

"I'll take two," I say. I'm out twelve bucks.

Now I wear a pair of Chinese, plain old hearing amplifiers the size, shape, and finish of a '65 VW Beetle, crap-brown in color with big brass bolts that stick out of the side of my head like Frankenstein's.

I step into the street traffic and realize two things: 1) I haven't heard well in years and 2) You people out there live in a noisy, raucous world. No wonder you are all nuts.

The rest of Burma, now that I can hear it, is a total surprise. All I'd known about it before we got there was that its name was changed to Myanmar when it was taken over by the army generals. Before that, it was a kingdom and, when the military seized power, they governed with their military mind, turning a poor country into a broken one, stealing everything: the teak, the land, the oil, and the gas, nonetheless, they seem unable to destroy the endless charm of the Burmese people.

The Irrawaddy River is like the Nile is for Egypt: both the pumping blood and the bony spine of the country. A flat, meandering stream a mile wide, and wider in places, narrows tightly in others, flowing along a river bed that is always shifting sand, the flowing current building then tearing down the underwater dunes. It makes for hazards that tax the talents of river pilots who come aboard and then depart every fifty miles. They look impassive but one can tell the pilots mostly guess at the most navigable channel, for the river is cream chocolate, and nothing under the surface is visible. In low water, as it is now, it can be running only inches deep, without a hint of danger on the surface. Running aground and bumping over bottom dunes is commonplace.

In high water, it can be many feet deep and several miles wide, flooding over farmland and replenishing the soil in its annual rush to the sea. Islands are built and destroyed in days, and large tracts of normally dry sand are left fertile when inundated by this mother-river.

On the river, there is ceaseless noise. The pounding of the single-cylinder diesel engines that drive the long tail boats sitting low in the water covers the visually peaceful scene with a raspy, nasty exhaust; both seem especially designed to invade one's head until you go mad. There is no place to hide from these 'one lungers' that power homemade trucks and tractors, and everything else that requires more than mere manpower. The constant thumping vibrates along the river day and night.

Away from the cities and towns there are no telephone land lines, there are no contrails in the sky, no airplanes. Farming is the same as it was a thousand years ago. Or three thousand. Yoked oxen pull plows and wooden harrows in their plodding, head-waving rhythm, the farmer behind watching his furrow and the unplowed ground ahead. Big bulls with swinging testicles plod along slowly in front of a rattletrap cart with surprisingly fine wooden wheels or old rubber tires while the driver sits atop the cart clucking to the bullocks. He starts at sunrise and works until the light fails. Everybody does.

At dawn, lines of women in conical hats tied down with scarves chatter away as they march to work on the day's rows, which stretch to infinity. Colorful longyi, sarong-like skirts, cover them from waist to foot. When the red of sundown comes, they quick-march home with their tools on their shoulders and become a living Communist poster, heroically working for pennies a day.

Tens of thousands of pagodas and temples dot the land, sticking up like teeth above the tree line, serrating the horizon—

stupas built to earn credits with the Buddha, to make up for wrong doing here on earth, an attempt to avoid being reincarnated as a rat or pig or cockroach. For the sinner, getting turned into a varmint is a one-way trip—once having achieved the low station through wrong doing, the sinner cannot ever recover their former shape as a human being. It sounds draconian but apparently inspires sinners to build pointy buildings and temples, which anyone can enter. Each shelter contains some holy relic of the Buddha, a hair, a fingernail clipping or some tiny, even infinitesimal body part. It seems the Buddha himself is spread pretty thinly around the countryside. The pagodas, which one cannot enter, are also impressive in their design and colorful testaments to the dissolute nature of their sponsor but Buddha must be pleased as he allows the pagodas all to stand unprotected.

We dock in a pint-sized town on the sandy banks of the Irrawaddy (pronounced Earwdeee) River. The other passengers are taking a tour in three passenger carts pulled by real small and under-motivated horses driven by ever smiling and over-motivated drivers. As rich white tourists, we are subjects of deep interest, so the natives stare at us, and we stare back.

I don't go with the rest. I hate being bombarded by the guides' incessant talk, about history that I am not interested in learning. My ADD kicks in and my eyes glaze over early in the blah-blah-blah. I'd rather photograph the locals.

So, I end up on the main drag which is filled with shops that sell everything plastic an Irawaddite (or is it Irawaddino?) could yearn for. There is much hustle and bustle, chatter, noise, and color.

I decide to shoot a rolling video clip of the main street. For three bucks I hire a man who will let me ride behind him on his motor scooter. I carefully explain that we'll ride one block, make a left at the first corner, go one block along the main street, make another left, then another, to return me to my starting place with my footage. One traveling shot. Three minutes. Simple.

We putt up the main street and come to the first left; he motions his clear intention to turn left, which he does in a wobbly way as I throw him off balance. At the second corner, I say, "Go left."

He doesn't. He goes straight, and we quickly transition from the bustling commercial town center to the seamy part where robbers and rapists hang out.

At the next corner, I say, "Turn left." He doesn't.

A few blocks later, down a dirt street, I say over his shoulder, "I want to go back to the boat."

He turns left.

Now we ride a couple of blocks past small dilapidated houses and women working and men lounging and curs with mange sleeping along the shoulder of the road.

My metal hip hurts now, and I know it ain't going to get any better. I say again, "I want to go back to the boat!"

He turns left.

We drive further out of town. I am now thoroughly confused as to where we are. Bouncing along on the pocked roads while holding the driver's shoulder with one hand and shooting video with the other puts my hip in a bad position. I try to scoot around on the seat to ease the pain, and a knife of hot steel stabs me in the butt.

I say with emphasis, "I want to go back to the goddam BOAT!"

He turns left.

I say, "Stop."

He does in front of a roadside tea shop.

Trying to dismount, my foot gets hung up on the driver's butt, and I am firmly trapped half on and half off the scooter. My hip is frying. My leg won't work. I can't get it unhooked. It is so seized up I can't even let go and fall to the ground. A young man walks out of the tea place, bodily picks me up and sets me on my feet. I thank him. He laughs. I ask him, "Which way is the boat?"

He points straight down this road that disappears into the trees. I raise my eyes to the bluest sky and thank Zeus. Great. Finally some solid information.

After walking around for a few minutes, my hip feels better; the hot pain is gone and has reduced itself to an ache. But I can make it back to the boat; I know where it is. I've been lost for an hour and seen much of the town and surrounding country side.

Back on the motor scooter, I point down the road and yell into the driver's ear, "Go straight ahead to the boat!"

He turns left.

I am starting to worry now. Words escape me. Is there something about the word 'boat?' Does boat mean 'left' in Burmese? When I try to speak, it all comes out gibberish. After three tries, I gag out, "English. I need to find someone who speaks English."

Magically, a golf course clubhouse appears. I yell "Stop!" I dismount painfully but unassisted and ask the lady there sitting in an open window, "Do you speak English?"

She stares at me like I am a ghost. "Do you speak English?" She turns and canvasses four or five other people in the room behind her. Heads fill the open window, and they all stare at me like an apparition.

Through another open window, a man hunches over his bookkeeping. There is a clean sheet of paper on his table. I grab the pen out of his hand and draw the outline of a riverboat. I hold it up like show-and-tell. Everyone looks at it. Giggles go around.

"I want to get back to my…" I just can't say the word. I rattle the sketch and, with force, repeat, "BOAT!…BOAT!…BOAT!"

"Ah," the woman says, her face brightening, "Come back to sheep! You come back to sheep!"

"Yes! Yes! That's it! Come back to sheep! Right now!" Solid information, finally, a clear direction. No more bullshit confusion between the words boat and left. Sheep.

My driver nods like he knew it all along. Doing my best impression of Marlene Dietrich I say, "I vant to go to dee sheep."

We drive directly to the river bank, and through the trees, I spot the sheep from a hundred yards away.

"This is good," I tell the driver. "I'll walk from here." He grins, I give him another thousand kyet tip, and I hobble down the bank. My hip is killing me.

They have moved the sheep. When I stepped ashore I videoed the trail up the bank and the garbage alongside. But this riverbank is clean. Well, it needed a good cleaning, I think. Clean is good for tourism.

Aboard, I am greeted by the sandal washing crew. As usual, they ask my cabin number. 316. They pick the numbered key from a hook and place on the top of my clean sandals, and I walk aft.

I video some men hauling sand in buckets from a small boat to a truck in a continuous line. It is very graphic and an iconic statement about the archaic state of Burma.

A man in a white ship's officer uniform whom I hadn't seen before walks quickly towards me, waving a paper, and with a big smile asks, "What is your name?"

I tell him.

Skimming down the clipboard, he asks ever politely, "What cabin are you in?"

"Cabin 316," I say.

With a pleasant smile, he says, "You are on wrong boat."

"Whadda ya mean? This is Pandaw Indochina isn't it?"

"Yes, but this Pandaw Indochina *Two*. You belong Pandaw Indochina *One*."

"So where the hell is Pandaw Indochina *One*?"

He points up the river. "Up there."

Recovering my sandals, the sandal washer hands me the key to cabin 316. I drop it in my pocket.

The Pandaw Indochina One sails at 11 AM. I am nearly a mile downriver from my boat. It is already three minutes past sailing time.

In all my years I have never been late for a sailing. Now I am going to miss my only lifeline to the free world. Iris will be seriously worried. God only knows where the nearest American Embassy is. Or even if there is one. Burma has only been open for two years. At the pace our government moves, I'll bet the embassy isn't even built yet; it's still a goddam hole in the ground and the Ambassador is living in a rattan hut in the middle of the excavation. I am stuck here, stranded in a nameless Burmese town, without walking around money in my pocket and no identification. My breath comes in short bursts.

I clamber up the sandy bank to the paved road.

If I walk, the boat is twenty minutes upriver. I know I can't make it before it leaves.

At the riverside bar on the bank, there is a line of parked motor scooters. I speak to a man standing outside with a beer. "Who owns those scooters?"

His thumb points into a darkened door. Men sit at the bar, drinking and laughing. As I walk in, heads swivel.

I make scooter noises, twist an imaginary throttle with one hand and hold out some bills in the other.

A half-drunk kid and his motor scooter weaves me the mile upstream to the boat.

And, as we ride along the river, I refuse even to think the word "boat" that seems to be interchangeable with "left."

Finally aboard my own boat, I go to the purser and explain that the key I am giving him opens cabin 316, but on Pandaw Two, not this boat.

He looks puzzled. "How did you get it?"

"Well, it's a long story. I went aboard the Pandaw Two." His eyebrows lift, and he grins.

"You got on the wrong boat?" He works and fails to hold back a belly laugh.

"Yeah. Ya see, I was on this motorcycle…"

He watches me squirm out of the corner of his eye, shakes his head and grins broadly.

"Oh… the hell with it," I say.

At the next dawn, I leave my cabin to get a morning coffee. A deck hand painting the deck looks up at me, his glowing white teeth slicing through a tawny brown face. He points at me with his brush, "Wrong boat!" he exclaims and bursts out laughing.

UNCLE HO

To the Viet Namese, Hanoi is two words—Ha' Noi—romanized for the ignorant westerner. The capital city is a churn of people, vegetables, a few cars and three million motor scooters that scream in tight shoulder-rubbing herds up and down the streets, dicing for position amidst raucous two-stroke exhaust noise. While waiting at traffic lights, the riders hyperventilate, impatiently gunning their engines in clouds of blue smoke. Alluring women, their sexy high heels hooked back over the foot pegs, mix with men in helmets and dark clothes, sitting expectantly on their mechanical mounts like an attacking army waiting to charge, orderly but anxious.

In order to cross the street in the midst of this maelstrom of wild Asians wheeling their smoking crotch-rockets, one has to step boldly off the curb into the whirling, deafening mass, choosing a walking speed that will carry you across the street without hesitation. You do not dare stop. You do not dare change pace. Any adjustment to your initial commitment will cause the river of speeding hot metal to wash over you like a sand ripple. Steady forward movement without hesitation, in spite of your fear, will cause the roaring sea to magically divide, to flow around you Moses-like, automatically adjusting to your foreigner's uncertainty, the flow continuing around you without a ripple. At the other curb, you turn and look back and marvel at your good luck, you survived.

For those of us still alive who observed the Viet Nam War (here they call it the American War), Hanoi was the center of North Viet Nam, a communist country politically owned by Ho Chi Minh. He connived, warred and slaughtered to wrest his country from the colonial French and the American presidents who felt that killing people from the North would stop the Communist dominoes that would surely fall across Asia. Ho is a legend who fought for thirty years to shake his country loose from the occupying forces of the French and the United States. His myth lives, vibrates really, for the Viet Namese who were not yet born in his time. They whisper his name reverentially. He is their George Washington.

Visiting the city without seeing Uncle Ho's Mausoleum is a crime against good judgment much like visiting Washington, DC and avoiding the Capitol. It just isn't done.

Ho's last resting place is a gray granite cube, big but not huge, standing alone in the middle of a park in the center of the city. Allegedly it is based on the design of Lenin's tomb, but in reality, there is no resemblance to Lenin's low, rectangular, red granite monolith in Red Square. Uncle Ho's five columns and square, three-story, simple tomb speaks of dignity without hubris and, depending on earthquakes, it should stand for five hundred years.

Our taxi stops several hundred yards away, at a big steel gate with a soldier on guard. We leave cameras, packs, and purses with our guide and shuffle to the narrow entrance and into a guard house. We proffer our tickets to a uniformed soldier who does not look at us and follow a pointing finger to a line of visitors where we are instructed about the protocols of a state visit. To wit: no cameras, no sunglasses, no caps, no shorts, no miniskirts, no talking, no purses, packs or bags, no exposed legs, two lines, no getting out of line, march two abreast, no hands in pockets, no smiling at the soldiers, no stopping. Other than these minimum constraints, there is little to indicate that this is still a military country.

On the hundred-yard march to the columned entrance across the concrete acreage that fronts the building, I step out of line just to test the disciplinary waters. It comes instantly: a yell from a soldier and his unmistakable motion that means "Get your white western ass back in line before I shoot your dick off!"

After climbing up a ramp, we step into a foyer filled with more soldiers who re-enforce the strict discipline about hands and hats and sunglasses. They bark with authority and cow us all into silence. We slowly shuffle around a corner and through an imposing brass door, into a darkened chamber. It takes a moment for our eyes to adjust to the half-light, then we realize we are in the room with HIM.

Uncle Ho lies in state inside a glass box, his head slightly raised so he can watch his visitors. His spotlighted face looks weird. Even so, he is fully in command, wearing a meticulously pressed and cleaned, high-collared military uniform. The whole magilla is raised on a dais that emerges from the floor below leaving a large open gap between us tourists and his glass box. We pace steadily around the three sides of the bier—no stopping and gawking, keep moving. Soldiers in the void beneath Ho are changing guard with a quiet, mechanical precision. We proceed slowly, steadily, in complete silence except for the shuffling of feet. The only other sounds emitted by the thirty or so folks in the chamber are the gentle slap of flip-flops. All heads are turned to the left, the Viet Namese staring at the small body of their savior, the rest of us simply staring. A spotlight shines on Ho's withered face, highlighting the startling color of his complexion. Then, suddenly, passing through a nondescript door, we are outside again under the gaze of the sun, back in the light and fresh air of the glorious day, instantly relieved to be away from death and the soldiers.

We stand and look across the square of grass and concrete and ponder what we have seen. Women in conical hats, on their hands and knees, pick at blades of grass growing in the sidewalk cracks. Without tools or gloves, they use their bare fingers.

I turn to Iris and say, "Who would have thought that their George Washington would be the color of a citrus fruit hanging from a tree in Florida? He is orange! Wow! Uncle Ho's face is bright orange!"

JERUSALEM W/O RELIGION

We enter the city, not via camel through the Eye-of-the-Needle but by a four-lane highway, in a modern bus with an indoor restroom and thirty-one other paying pilgrims.

The Old City is just that: old, with visiting hordes creeping shoulder-to-shoulder through the choked streets, the foot traffic occasionally gridlocks, seizes stock still, belly-to-butt, waiting for the unseen people ahead to move on.

Ten different religions vie for supremacy here, the Jews are just one sect that believe they own the only true God, but each of the sects believes in myths worth dying for.

The moderns live cheek by jowl with the ancients; the ancient part of the city is surrounded by sleek modern cubist buildings and neighborhoods that march up and down the hills in ranks.

In today's political environment, sometimes one stands on Israeli land and then, just a few yards away, on Palestinian turf. Who owns what is carefully mapped, defended, endlessly argued over and, eventually, will be fought over again. True believers will again die for their myths, battling over the turf that their private God said, by Heavenly decree, was rightfully theirs.

We are standing on the Mount of Olives in the Palestinian area overlooking the Old City. The golden Dome of the Rock sticks up like a shiny bald head above the hustle of the gritty neighborhoods and can easily be hit with a bullet from a high-powered rifle.

The Jewish cemetery, laid out just below us, is covered by acres of casket-shaped white boxes. Our guide tells us the dead themselves are seven feet below the surface. The stark white oblong boxes used to be regularly raided at night by the Palestinians, but now there is a cop walking the dead beat.

Over there, a few hundred yards away in the Old City, Jerusalem is disappointing. I expected glory and found sweaty crowds, moribund myths, ancient stones falling apart from age, and smelly tourists. It's just another dirty Arab hilltop town that has been fought over for five thousand years.

Historically, governments here change with predictable regularity. Since Year Zero, there have been 27 different governments. On direct orders from their god, the Jews have considered Israel the Jewish homeland since the tenth century. Then they found that in this fractious neighborhood there is a big difference between deciding they own it and getting the neighbors to agree to the new property lines. Every different religion casts envious eyes and thinks it is theirs, too. They invade and keep it for a while and then lose it in the name of the next ambitious god. During its long history, Jerusalem has been destroyed twice, besieged 23 times, attacked 52 times, and captured and recaptured 44 times. In the past 2100 years, countries, borders, governments and governors came and went in this part of the world. And all of this for a dingy, exhaust-choked, overcrowded city that no reasonable atheist could live in because there is no place to park. Truly, governments here are just penciled in, but the citizens live in denial about these historical facts. They also deny what the future inevitably holds for them.

If you remove the idea that big, dramatic religious feats happened here, and its ghostly participants still hang around today, the city is just one of thousands of piles of ancient rocks that dot the Middle East.

Like Disneyland, the business of the town is maintaining and keeping the myths real so that the faithful can connect directly to their ancient gods. Gods? Yes. While they talk about one god, a tourist gets the impression that there is a whole room full of them standing around in long fancy dresses. You get to take your pick about whose hem you cling to in the hopes of saving your miserable and sinful butt.

There is a constant bickering about which god is the real one; it's like picking the lead singer out of a Greek chorus. Nobody can tell objectively who is who and who has the power. They all stand opposite each other and yell "I am the rightful owner of this pitiful desert hilltop, and as the most humble servant in town, you can trust me on this one thing. Look how righteous I am! Give me money!"

The Via Dolorosa is just wide enough for two loaded donkeys to pass and lined with shops selling religious souvenirs and the ubiquitous tee-shirts that announce "America, Israel can protect you."

The street where Jesus mythically walked is marked by places where, it is believed, Jesus carried the cross. Not a cross as learned in Bible school. It was more likely a straight wood beam, a cross arm, just a simple piece of shaped timber with a hole in it designed to fit on the peg of a fixed upright post: the beam bearing the attached victim would be lifted and dropped onto the peg forming a T shape. After death, the beam was easily removed and reused, no fuss, no batteries required.

On the Via Dolorosa we are told 'Here is the place he first falls, there is the place where Jesus meets his mother'—and we're shown a dozen more notable stops in his march to his end. The pious ask to walk where Jesus walked, but this isn't possible since that hallowed ground is twelve feet below the current street.

A few blocks away from Dome of the Rock, which is currently under the control of the Muslims, the Church of Holy Sepulchre goes back to the 4th century and looks every year of it. Cobbled together over millennia, it is nearly falling down and needs continuous patching; it has been an important pilgrimage site since its beginning. The myth says this is where Jesus was nailed to the cross. He was prepared for burial here and he was buried here.

The tale is that this church was built on the Hill of Calvary—Golgotha—"Place of the Skull," where Christ was crucified and then buried nearby. The story is tough to verify though, since these facts were invented 300 years after his passing.

And recently, 'they' just opened Jesus' tomb inside the church, slid aside a ponderous slab, and found nothing beneath it except broken rocks. So much for collecting his DNA to learn which of us fundamentalist American Christians are direct descendants. Had that actually happened, it is likely CNN would interview a wrecker-driver in Amarillo, a Mexican illegal coincidently named Jesus, to find out what happened to his great-uncle twenty-five generations removed. Underneath the slab there was no bleached, grinning skull if one ever existed. What better way to bamboozle fearful believers than to bury a myth out of sight and call it holy when nothing can be confirmed or denied, only believed. (In Amarillo, Jesus had a billboard on the interstate that read "Troubles? Call Jesus." and he would show up with his tow-truck.)

In 326, Helena, so the story goes, the daughter of Emperor Constantine, searched for and found what she was sure was the true cross, buried for three centuries, birthing a myth that is famous in the Catholic faith. Splinters of it were scattered to the faithful worldwide to be revered, worshiped and worn inside lockets strung around believer's necks.

The three major religions, Christians, Jews, and Muslims share this same building.

The Stone of Anointing, where it is said Christ was prepared for burial, is a tourist highlight of the church. The believers kneel and caress the ordinary looking limestone slab. Their reverence is touching, and one can't help but admire the shining faces and the purity of their unshakable belief that this very stone supported the body of Jesus. The slab currently in use replaced the original, which broke and was reset by this new model in 1200AD. Oh, well, we don't want to let perfect get in the way of the good.

Jesus' tomb is a black cube twenty feet square and high, called the Edicule. It is contained within a highly decorated but dark, dark room. It is currently under renovation and tightly wrapped by steel scaffolding, perhaps all that's holding it together. The room is so crowded one can only creep along with the mass of silent and worshipful Christians shuffling by. The tranquility is broken continually by the various guides out-shouting each other, screaming their personal version of the story of Jesus as if they had walked beside him and, with their own strong arms, picked him up off the pavement after he fell.

Joke: The church leaders of the Muslims, Jews, and Christians walk into a bar and sit at the same table. Each order a different kind of drink. The bartender serves a single glass and sets it down between them. The ensuing argument and bar fight leave them all bloodied. The glass is filled with sand.

If you think I am a cynic, read Mark Twain on his visit here in 1867.

If one has no affinity for religious myths or attachments to Christians or Muslims or Greeks or Mormons or whoever, Jerusalem is not worth coming to visit.

My conclusion: if you want to visit a mythical land, visit Mickey, Minnie and Goofy in Orlando. It's cheaper. And cleaner. And a lot more fun.

ISTANBUL and BEYOND

Istanbul! The very name conjures up intrigue, glamor noir, turbans, long curved knives, murder on dark streets. But then reality intrudes. Istanbul is a big city overflowing with men in cars yelling at each other, muezzins yodeling five times a day from minarets around town working hard to be heard over each other, feral cats yowling, street vendors hawking and politicians in big sound trucks blaring unintelligible messages to an uninterested public. There is little to no laughing. It is not a happy populace. It is Muslim.

Muslim means a man's world with few women on the street. The restaurants are filled with men, the outdoor cafes and storefronts sport only men, dour, unsmiling men in gray or black clothes, staring impassively at the street scene, paying particular attention to the women visiting from the West who, in the eyes of these men, are all willing, libidinous, easy women in skirts and slacks who promise sex on demand without romance or foreplay or refusal, each and every one a crazed nymphomaniac.

The city is 2500 years old which assumes that a certain patina has been appliquéd by history, a civilization fully matured with architecture to match. But, with few exceptions, there is no patina, no historical hangover or scattered historic thrills for the tourist cum amateur historian. The city is like any modern city with high-rises, contemporary apartment blocks, and inner-city four-story residential buildings slowly dying from deferred maintenance and, while doing so, looking trashy. Nearly three thousand mosques dot the hills. The elaborate ones, even the biggest one in the world, are all squat, gray and bumpy, and look like large bug-eyed frogs. The back streets are one or two vehicles wide filled with fast cars driven by skillful but scary pilots who virtually shave pedestrians and, horns blasting, face each other down at intersections.

The place has a down vibe. Even in the most crowded sidewalk bistros, there is rarely a smile. But when you ask for directions, the locals happily answer with a smile and a gentleness that is unexpected. They will enthusiastically give you directions in detail even if their directions are wrong, which they usually are, but you leave happy and so do they. Hands across the sea and all that...

The Muslim world is a dramatically different one from the Christian world. Where Christianity has prevailed, there is usually laughter and smiles and nods in return for yours; beers and wines populate outdoor tables with men in intimate discussions with women who smile back and laugh and agree.

In the Muslim world, many women cover themselves with layers of clothes, headscarves or dead-black burkas from head to toe, many looking like crows. The young women with headscarves are fashion statements, their heads beautifully wrapped brightly colored packages of modesty, they click quickly down the streets in fashionable shoes giving all men a wide berth. The black crows tend to be Arabs visiting the city. Their husbands are young and fit and prosperous looking and often push baby carriages and yell orders and intimidate everyone around them. Again, no smiles.

Bulgaria is a broken Orthodox Christian country that barely survived the care, custody, and control of Communism. It remains in the throes of an economic and emotional hangover from those desperate years of Moscow's command economy.

The women dress in western style, but poorly. Neither men nor women look you in the eye. They don't nod in answer to your friendly nod. It is as if you did not exist and they don't want you to.

It is a big empty, green land with few people left on the farms. The fields still have that corporate look, miles, and miles of carefully delineated rectangles, a patchwork quilt created by people who could only sew square seams. The farmland is without people; they moved to the cities when their lands were taken by the state. When the property was returned to them, two decades later, they were too old to be interested in the drudgery of farming. The youngest third left the country for better opportunities to nurture their ambition and education elsewhere.

Vukovar, Croatia, this pretty town along the Danube, is nearly all new. In1991, in a stretch of eighty-seven days, it was reduced to dust by a million bombs and artillery projectiles, so the town is now composed of either new buildings or old falling bullet-riddled ones. And they sit side by side on the downtown streets, some used and some used up, the crumbling remnants of an internecine war.

This part of the world, Serbia, Croatia, Kosovo, Bosnia, the detritus of a collapsed Yugoslavia, shows the wear and tear of disastrous wars between differing and different countrymen. It has been that way for centuries, tribal alpha-dogs fighting it out to own the approaches to rivers and money and power, whole countries coming and going like quickie lovers at a country dance.

Even as a tourist, it is easy to see that ex-Yugoslavia is still broken ground generations after the death of Marshall Tito who held the country together by the ever-present threat of death by bullet.

Bucharest, Romania, however, is the polar opposite of Istanbul. The people are happy, look each other in the eye, (yes, even yours), drink wine, laugh at jokes, talk loudly, flirt with women and squeeze them close. The Friday afternoon hot spots overflow, the streets vibrate with a national joy of life in the sunset light that wedges down the streets of the Old Town. After Istanbul, the relief is palpable, washing over one's skin, releasing it from the cultural jail of Turkey. One walks easily in these streets, with people who obviously love life and live it fully. They give us all hope.

MANVAR DESERT CAMP

It was decided by the person in charge of scheduling that we would spend a couple of nights at a desert camp sleeping in a tent. I immediately thought of previous desert nights in Utah, sleeping on the ground in a pup tent. Of getting a cramp in my ass in the middle of the night which makes me get up and crawl into the cold darkness, dodging scorpions and other unseen dangers, while trying to find my boys which have shrunk beyond salvation from the cold night air.

I had no idea that the Indian version of a tourist desert camp included three meals a day under a dining tent the size of a four-car garage. A lined white sleeping tent. One of thirty shelters set in a circle, with a performance stage in the middle. That stage hosts native performers every evening at seven-thirty, whom we watch while sitting on sand covered by luxurious rugs and pillows. Camels lie around, posing proudly; the whole scene becomes a Christmas card sans snow.

Settling into this primitive camp, I first recharged my laptop from the floor plug, then I took a hot shower in the stone-lined bathroom. The windows are scalloped in the Jaipur Style, and the floor is polished sandstone. The beds are deep with many great quilts that smell good.

This remote and seemingly temporary little village resides in a low depression surrounded by high sand dunes, and feels very distant from the loud squalor of India until one walks to the crest of the nearest dune. Just on the other side of the sand piles are homes and goats and people and camels as far as the eye can see, in every direction, with plastic sheets flapping in the breeze and ever present trash blowing around. We are in the middle of a settlement.

So Iris and I sit on our sunny little porch in beach chairs, whiling away the hours in our sandy and remote location. I am sparkling clean from my hot shower and writing this on my newly recharged laptop. The refreshment walla is on his way down from the main lodge with a coffee refill. We have already perused the breakfast menu; it is full American and full Indian. There are extra rolls of downy soft toilet paper for Iris, right there by the flush potty.

Life is good. Ah, wilderness!

CALCUTTA CRICKET

Iris is asleep upstairs. An important cricket match is unfolding at one-quarter speed on a muted widescreen television—the Indian bartender and I watch a group of men in white stand around on a grass playing field.

Silently I revisit the question I have asked myself for years: How is cricket played?

Operating under the assumption that he is an expert who has explained the game to hundreds of half-loaded tourists, I ask the bartender, "How do you play and score this sport? There aren't any uprights or nets or courts or anything."

He is obviously delighted to have someone to talk to and admire his world-class knowledge about the game that migrated around to India with the Raj.

In a heavy accent, he begins, "It is played by two teams, one on each end of a lawn court. The object is to get the ball by the flatbatter and knock the girdle off the widker, those three vertical sticks with two short girdles placed on top. A tall man runs up to the line and with all his power, throws the ball really, really hard. The flatbatter tries to hit the ball, and, if he keeps the ball from hitting the three sticks and their girdles, the flatbatter runs dragging his flatbat about forty feet to the other end of the playing field and then back."

To demonstrate, the bartender takes off running down the bar room, turns around, and runs back toward the television, dragging his imaginary bat.

"That foot sprint is worth six runs." Holding up the correct number of fingers, he nods side to side and gives me a broad smile.

"If the ball goes over a berm in the outfield, that out-of-bounds is worth one run. If it stays inside, it is worth three and a half runs unless the ball touches the ground within ten meters of the flatbatter, in which case it is worth eight runs. This score is called a perso, which, in the overall scoring, is called a craddie. The number of craddies by itself doesn't win the squark; it takes at least a quardy within the mopo to back up the kuarned. That configuration is, in toto, called a snodd and very hard to accomplish, which is why cricket players are so highly paid, enjoy world fame, and consort with spectacularly beautiful women and fast cars, at least in India and a few other civilized countries, too. There aren't many other civilized countries, you know."

"However, the last flatbatter can snatch victory from the jaws of defeat if he pulls a maneuver called an edgy, where the ball is hit with the narrow side of the flatbat, goes over the boundary and into the expensive seats (that's called a "freebott') and the winner takes all. Unless the freebott is deemed illegal."

Now I must confess this was the only part I didn't understand. Perhaps it was lost in the bartender's accent. Evidently, a freebott is a very rare and risky tactic, and its success can cause something of a row among the spectators. In the most recent match between India and Sri Lanka, it caused a death by kicking, so freebotts are serious stuff. Police have to be on the field when an attempt is made. The game stops while the cops drive in from downtown, escorting an ambulance, and onto the court, lights flashing. It is very exciting and the spectators in the stands close their picnic baskets, quit chewing, stub out their cigarettes and pay attention, perhaps for the first time in six hours.

There you have it in its simplest form. As you may have correctly deduced by now, there are many more technicalities at the professional level that are too detailed to explore here.

I finish my drink and sign the bill.

On the TV, the game is shaping up into a craddie.

"Do you think they will have a freebott?" I ask.

The bartender doesn't look up. "No, Sir. It's too dangerous."

It was worth every penny to have this complicated game explained to me so simply. I'm now a huge fan. I'm going to go upstairs and explain it all to Iris.

I yell back from the doorway. "GO INDIA!"

LONDON

Stepping out of the Strand Palace Hotel, wet London hits me in the face. I watch the colors in the reflecting sidewalk streaming from people dodging umbrellas, coping with the falling rain, creating a symphony of sympathetic colors, a visual conversation between strangers hurrying along to work or love or desperation or just hurrying because that's what one does in London of a rainy morning.

The scene is so moving that I realize, or re-realize, how beautiful the world is—it makes me maudlin and feel exposed to see it all again. At my age, and as a photographer with sixty years of experience, I know the world, its images, its color, its failings, its very being, and while there are the constant rumbles of death and disaster, there is also the lingering beauty of recurring memories: fine people now passed on, fine cigars and fine loves, past victories and heartbreaking defeats, all in color and in rhythm and moving to life's irregular beat.

In the National Art Gallery, I see a small bent figure with pure silver hair wearing a tan raincoat, leaning on her cane, her back to me. I tap her on the shoulder and she turns quickly. Her face is a pure British matron's face. She smiles broadly and I say, "We have the same color hair!"

"We certainly do!" she says with a hearty laugh. Her cheeks flush pink and she says, "My name is Olive Hughes." We shake. Her hand is tiny and fragile. She is at least eighty.

"Well, Olive, you are a gorgeous woman!"

"Why, thank you so much!" she says with surprise.

We laugh together in the instant intimacy of the moment. She turns and walks away giggling. I am moved to tears by her soul, a lovely solid statue encased in fragile aging flesh.

Surrounded by great paintings, the transcendent images of my life are still vivid and fully alive decades after being seen and absorbed into the coarse weave of my soul. They are the colors of London in the rain.

GALAPAGOS

The mellow Equatorial wind drifts across the fantail of our anchored tour boat, a black and white fifty-year-old vessel, her hollow sides and standout ribs exposed by years of random collision with the unlimited power of attacking waves.

The water laps around the hull with gentle, sensual slaps and taps. Wavelets rise to resist the breeze and march in ranks across the surface of the sea now yielding itself to the oncoming rain that veils the island.

A pacific spot in the Eastern Pacific, Galapagos is the true end of the world. Six hundred miles from the Ecuadorian coast, it floats in the ocean, far removed from mainland stability and easy access.

The islands themselves aren't much: low and volcanic, products of the continuous shift of earth's birth canal across the ocean floor where she pushed out gray, red, and black ash cones and slathers of black lava. In creation-time, some of that happened just yesterday. On the sides of the latest eruptions, green fills every foot right down to the buff sand beach.

Giant tortoises as big as truck tires live inside that green, humped round and hard like overinflated soccer balls, dark and patterned and worn, heads sticking out like snorkels, round knobs pinned to wrinkled necks, whole dark spheres walking with painful slowness, a foot here…then a foot there…
foot here…
      foot there…
           here…
                there…
                      the achingly slow walk of the aged…

They mind their own deliberate business with an enviable ability to concentrate on their route of march, their food, their lover, ignoring the tall interlopers who loved and admired them and took them sailing away on whaling ships along with thousands of their hard-shelled relatives to be fed to the hunters of whales. Because they stored well and could live for a year in the tropical heat without food or water. Until eaten, however, life for the tortoise is heaven, a paradise of endless food and freedom to live and love and have babies as they please in this protected archipelago.

Black-and-white wooden stakes show visitors how far they can invade their paradise, how far up the beach, where the trail goes, the margins of the iguana's nesting grounds, the limits of the city gawkers.

The birds of sailor jokes, blue footed boobies, fly fast and low, then, climbing higher, spotting fish below, fold into a wingless spear, and pierce the water at lightning speed with hardly a ripple. The fish don't have a chance when these fleet birds are on the prowl, peeling off like fighter planes, one behind the other in a speeding, staccato arch, dive bombing, plunging a split second apart into the unseen schools below.

Sea turtles and sharks rule the transparent sea; tropical fish flash tribal colors in both attacks and escape; sea lions, slick brown lumps, loll for a living in the water and on the beaches, sleep like logs, impervious to the wet drops falling from broken skies.

The sporadic rain floats soundlessly in, covering the tourist fleet at anchor in a misty half-seen world. It is quiet except for the splash and churn of waves against the hull. Water meets steel. The canopies suspended above deck, collect the rain into pools which spill dramatically with the ship's roll, a transparent crash of hundreds of gallons of fresh water.

Long ago, rain was a blessing for sailors who jealously stored it in casks. They stood naked while this pure gift of the heavens cleansed them of the salt trapped in their pores and released the sticky sweat that had leathered their skin, and rinsed clothes that had not dried for days. Because salt holds water close to its bosom it never releases its love-grip until melted by fresh water from the sky. Water that wets and cleanses scabs, freshens the decks and lines and all topside surfaces, the sails, the halyards, the stays and blocks. Everything and everyone turns fresh again, after the wetting and the release of the enemy of comfort: ocean salt. A freshwater rinsing at sea is being reborn.

The tropics are mostly benign but sometimes, in a fit of pent-up rage, destroy both man and beast's carefully tended nests, killing the earth's surface dwellers with vicious wind swirls and waves as high as city buildings, determined to fulfill the suicidal desire of every ship to sink and rest comfortably on the bottom of the sea. Ah the sea: that unreliable mistress, dangerously unfaithful, given to warm deceptions and fickle tempers. The mood this morning is gray. Vessels at anchor hobbyhorse at their chains, waiting for orders from their masters, all the while yearning for rest and the silent, quiet peace that inevitably awaits them on the rocky bottom.

ON MY BACK

I am fixing my decorative yard lights. The outside timer has failed, and they no longer come on at sundown. I am on my knees and the big plants are crowding me, trying to push me off the top of the wall, make me fall, make me hurt myself. It is a conspiracy of nature and balky electricity, with a hint of crazy. I am obsessed with having the lights work. These are the things one worries about at 78—whether the goddam lights work the way they are supposed to.

Frustration and pain are both building in me. My knees hurt, my thigh muscles are cramped. The tiny screw that must fit into the two electrical lugs is misaligned and won't slide through, making a straight course into the threaded hole. After twenty failures in a row, my glasses fall off my nose. I can no longer stand this crouched and cramped position, and my hip joint hurts like hell. I struggle to stand up. The world twirls and I grab for a nearby tree limb to steady myself. The wind is blowing twenty, maybe thirty. Everything in my garden is in motion. I have no balance left.

I think about calling Iris out to steady me. But that would be yielding to the wind, the wall, the big plants, the frustration of the uncooperative screw and its evil companions, the electrical lugs. I won't yield to such conditions, even though my body groans. My legs quiver, 'getting their shake on' someone once called it. The sound of the wind takes me back to another place altogether:

Teenager. Winter. Late afternoon. The wind, gusting to forty. Twenty or thirty below zero. Casper, Wyoming. On my back.

It is a brutally hard winter in 1948. I'm living with my father in a twenty-three-foot Alma aluminum trailer-house on the far edge of a deserted mobile home park, the last lonely trailer out there where the nearest neighbor is open ground as far as one can see. The ground blizzard blowing snow fifty feet into the air obscures everything more than twenty feet away. There's nothing to break the wind. Snow streaks snake across the scrubbed hardpan. It is a world of utter whiteouts, unrelenting cold, and the ice-hardened desert floor.

A person can freeze to death in thirty minutes in this wind. And people do, after their cars stall on a back road, stuck in a snow drift. Idling the engine to keep the heater on, they run out of gas while praying for the snow plow that will save them. The cold wind converts the automobile into a refrigerator. The family huddles for warmth and, without talking, they go to sleep. And their bodies shut down, the kids' little bodies freeze first. The automobile disappears under a fast building white drift in the middle of the scoured clean black pavement. A fog of snow swirls up and over the shoulder of the road and forms a curling wave that blinds every living thing.

A rancher making his way from the barn back to his warm kitchen hugs a fence post against the wind gusts and freezes rigid fifty yards from his back door. The cattle herd for warmth, huddling in depressions, the smothering white snow drifts solid over them and blankets their world—they die together. A calf, caught open to the blizzard, builds a snout of ice that grows so heavy he can't hold up his head, and when the ice-muzzle inexorably touches the ground, it freezes there, anchoring him still, standing in his dying place until the thaw. All of this takes place within twenty minutes; the calf now a five-legged statue in the middle of nowhere, the rancher becoming just an extra post, the car a snowdrift.

I lie on my back underneath the trailer, working to unstop a hard-frozen drain hose. My daddy ordered me to unstop it so I must. The only option is to quit, go inside, get warm, and take the leather belt for failing again.

I chip away at the ice blockage with a dull screwdriver. No good. A chip here flipping off downwind, another chip, then eventually another. Eighteen minutes into this project I am sweating hard, and beginning to chill. The cold, which had been tolerable for a few minutes, is now deadly. It is well below zero. The frozen snot that gathered and then melted in my nose is no longer melting. The desert land is barren everywhere except that behind every bush or rock, each obstruction, no matter how small, a V-shaped, long-tailed snowdrift has formed, exactly proportional to the size of the obstacle. The only thing left on the bare ground is gravel; any dirt has long since raced south in snaking tendrils to Colorado, carried by sandblasting winds, flying snow and the Arctic weather.

Gusts shake the trailer as it dams up against it then splits, some going above and some driven below, creating a physical force that kills everything it touches.

I work the screwdriver around the drain, but it slips and does nothing. The icy lip is up inside the drain; it refuses to give way. There are inches to go to release the water trapped above which, when it is finally released, will fall onto my face. I look forward to that, to having that dirty, cold water dump into my face and deliver my reprieve from this hell. For then I can get warm.

I feel lost. Only my daddy knows where I am. I have no friends. I have never met my mother. I live alone in my mind, and I am worthless, a gap filler, a zero, useless to the world. During my thirteen years, my daddy has cursed my uselessness hundreds of times. What difference does it make if I freeze out here? No one can see me underneath in the drifts; I won't be found until sometime tomorrow and then only if the wind stops. That's okay with me. The wind whips my tears away and blowing snow forms a layer of ice on my face. A drift is quickly building behind me.

I chip away at the ice but after a time I lie back and just look at the bottom of the trailer, inches from my face, watch the talcum snow blur by, stare at my enemy, the frozen blob in the drain pipe. I feel the sneaking cold. My eyelashes stick together, and I pry them apart. The shivering has stopped and now I feel almost comfortable, even a bit warm. Sleepy.

I listen to the howl that drives the gravel stinging through my pants leg. I jerk awake. I know what is happening. My hands can't grip the screwdriver. It's fallen down on the ice. I can't pick it up. I am freezing.

Stiffly, I slide out from under the trailer and stand up. My legs wobble and don't want to work, but I force them. I can't feel my hands. I can't feel my feet. I can't feel my face beneath the ice coat. I have to quit the job and pay with pain. I give up.

It always goes like this, I think, with the sinking feeling of facing him.

The wind screams without rest.

…the wind…the icy wind…the burning wind…

The screw finally submits and rotates the lugs into place. The lights come on. I put my tools away and go inside and fix myself a drink.

Listening to the eternal wind, I say to Iris, "The yard lights work."

She smiles her extraordinary smile.

BOY

The boy hated Sunday. The Old Man never worked on Sunday, and the boy spent Sundays with him, tolerating, dodging the lightning hands that flashed with little warning, hitting his ear or cheek or jaw. The Old Man had been a prizefighter, and his aim was spot on. His hands were tough, blunt and lumpy around the knuckles from years of laying brick and landing punches. He was medium height, round in the chest, as thick through as across and slightly stooped in the shoulders. Easy hazel eyes and prematurely gray hair, a broad-set mouth and thin lips made him look particularly benign. His appearance belied his strength; his head sat forward on his shoulders, adding to the deception.

The Old Man had been angry for years. Today's anger started at breakfast. The boy didn't mind the beatings so much as he did the scorn the Old Man piled onto him; the words hurt him inside. If he had to choose between the old man's fists and his words, Boy feared his words the most. He had learned that his boy's body would pretty much heal by the next Sunday if he stayed clear of fast hands during the week.

The Colorado summer sun warmed the aluminum trailer house. It was a short, roundish trailer with a bed in the back and a couch in the front. In the middle were a small galley, cabinets and a closet. There was no bathroom. With the trailer court space rental came the right to use the communal bathroom across the gravel drive. The garbage cans were over there too, and the laundry room. The trailer was crowded for two people, and, like in a small boat, they had to indicate what they were going to do and turn together to move around inside. There was no place to hide.

The Old Man had run out of milk at breakfast. His fury was building. "The next time I run out of milk I'm gonna whip you 'til you piss like a dog." His mouth was tight in the corners, a bad sign; he would find other things wrong.

The boy was wary. "Yes, Sir. I didn't think you'd use so much." Hard time would start soon.

"Think? Think? Who the hell said that you could think?" The Old Man peered around the tiny space. His gaze circled and lit like a fly on a grease spot behind the stove. "I thought I told you to clean up this goddam place."

"Yes, sir, I thought I did," the boy said weakly.

The Old Man stood quickly and in one step had the boy by the ear. He pointed the boys head using his ear as an arrow, dragging the slightly built lad.

"Do you see that? What's that?"

"It's grease, Sir."

"Grease. What's it doing there?" The words came out sideways, contempt easing their way, letting them slide together.

Boy resigned himself. His dark brown eyes clouded. "I don't know, from the eggs I guess; I don't know." His ear hurt, and he yielded to the pressure of the knobby knuckle jamming behind it, distorting his neck.

"You don't know? You don't know." When the old man's voice dropped, it was always followed by a punch. This one was a short one cutting up from the inside. It landed on the son's cheekbone, and his knees went away; he fell to the floor, back against the bed.

"Get up you good-for-nothing." The boy squirmed, spinning away from the sharp toed cowboy boot. He knew he had a chance; the Old Man was not good with his feet. "Get up and clean this filthy place up."

The Old Man flopped down on the plaid couch. He flushed with anger and combat and frustration. "God, if you were a man I'd whip your ass till you couldn't walk. You are a no-good just like your cousin, Jimmy."

Cousin Jimmy came up at times like this. Boy had never known him but had a picture of him in his mind, about his size but a sneak thief and a liar and a coward, a hateful person especially hated by the Old Man. The boy hated him, too and felt cheap and embarrassed when the Old Man compared them.

"You're gonna to end up just like him—in reform school. That whole damned family was trashy. White trash."

That whole family was the boy's mother's family. The Old Man had stolen him from his mother at gunpoint. Something about an Appalachian Mountain misunderstanding that had turned into a blood feud.

"If I hadn't been a dead shot with a thirty-five Remington, your uncles would have killed me. They even tried to get me one time, but I faced 'em down. Caught me hunting ground hogs out on the back road to Mount Airy," the Old Man said. The boy always wondered why, if the Old Man disliked him so much, he had stolen him when he was two years old in the first place. It was a puzzle.

"Get the hell up and start cleaning."

"Yes, Sir."

"Get a pan and some soap and water and clean that damned woodwork."

The boys heart sunk. The whole interior was woodwork and, except for the floor and the windows at each end, it was varnished plywood.

"All of it, Sir?"

"You goddam right all of it, every last little goddam bit of it."

The boy started behind the stove, working and watching the Old Man who lay on the couch reading the paper. In time, the paper fell forward, and he dozed off.

The boy slowed but kept scrubbing, sweating in his dirty undershirt. He worked up over the icebox but didn't open the door. He knew what horrors of mold and rot hid in there and dreaded the smells that attacked when the door containing that wildness opened.

He had cleaned and cooked and laundered for the Old Man since he was eleven. He had grown up on the road, in cars and tents and motel rooms and he had been boarded out to people. He was always a visitor. He once lived with his aunt in a lovely home in Berkeley, but when the Old Man bought a trailer house, the boy was ready to move on from the rigid life and had come back to live with him, away from the stark neatness of the suburbs. He was glad to be back with the Old Man. Then the anger started with the fists and belts and wet washrags.

The boy feared the wet washrag. When spun and snapped, it stung and bit deep into skin and muscle. With fists and belts, he could sometimes blunt and partially avoid the blows with his arms, hands, and elbows, protecting his face and tender midsection, down around the kidneys and belly. But the washrag was a snake, feinting and striking late, the timing off, whistling like a stick but bending, then coiling, around hands and fingers, burning and tearing inside the skin. Somehow, it tore at the joints and hurt deeper inside, and they swelled up.

Some of his fingers weren't working now, growing stiff. The first time he was wounded he had put on a splint made out of an ice cream stick and white tape, but the Old Man tore it off. The boy never splint a torn joint again. It was too noticeable, and it made the Old Man mad. Eventually, the joints stopped hurting real bad, but they stayed fat and stiff and sore.

After an hour, the Old Man strangled in his sleep, spit caught in his throat, sucked down in reaction to a dream, and he gagged and rolled over and sat up in a fit of coughing that shook the trailer. His face and eyes were red with the unexpected work. He coughed for a time, his eyes finally focusing on the now quickly moving youth scrubbing the cabinets below the sink.

"What's taking you so goddam long?" The man's voice was deep with sleep.

"I don't know sir. I'm working as fast as I can." It was a lie, but it was going to be a rough day anyway. There was no way out of it.

Standing, the Old Man exploded. "The hell you say!" The boy ducked away from an open backhand, but it caught enough of his head that the man didn't feel avoided. The father stepped outside and stood by his black Lincoln with the chrome air horns mounted on the hood. He called back through the screen door, "Get me some ice water."

The boy felt the fear box up in his stomach. Ice water meant ice. Ice meant icebox. There was no ice. It meant the Old Man might look into the cooler and see its bad smelling colors. He would really raise hell then.

"We don't have any ice, sir." he said weakly.

The man wheeled in the gravel, moved inside and jerked open the icebox door. Repulsive smells filled the hot air.

He slammed the door. "You no good white trash. How many times have I told you to keep this clean?"

"I don't know, sir."

"Then why didn't you do as you were told?"

"Cause I forgot." The boys voice shook.

"Forgot? Forgot? Well, I'll teach you to forget." The Old Man's temper showed as red skin.

"You're trash, just like your cousin Jimmy." The Old Man pulled a gray washcloth from a drawer handle and ran water on it from the tap and without wringing it, began.

The boy was already shrinking away, crying and pleading, hunting for the corner by the closet where a full swing would be difficult. "Please Daddy, don't whip me. I'll keep it clean; I promise I will…I'll keep it clean."

"You damned well bet you will." The dreaded cloth looped and struck and looped again, coming in flatly, off the timing, encircling his flailing hands and forearms, then snapping, stinging and bruising deeply, driven by the full force of mature muscle.

The boy screamed, whimpered and cried again as the serpent poised and coiled in the air and struck.

"Shut up, goddam it; I'll teach you to scream." The Old Man murmured. The boy moved in tight to get inside the arc of the snake, his nose almost on the mans shirt pocket. The man surprised his adversary with a short, flashing left hook. The boy never saw it.

When he awoke, his head hurt fiercely. He lay on the bed sideways, his feet dangling over the edge. The Old Man stood away from him watching him closely through narrowed eyes. Then he muttered, "From now on when I tell you to do something, you do it."

"Yes, Sir."

The Old Man turned and stepped down through the narrow doorway and was gone. The boy heard the Lincoln start and drive away.

He began to heave deep sobs starting from below his belt-line. After a time his sobbing eased, leaving his chest muscles tired and a jerking in his belly. He sat on the edge of the bed and thought about what to do. He had a headache, and his face hurt. There was a lump on his jaw. He looked at the welts on his arms and stomach. Two fingers were swelling again. How long had it been? A year ago, maybe two, back then he had hoped there was a chance the Old Man's mood might get better. It was getting worse. There seemed to be no end to it. He didn't understand what made the Old Man so mad. Maybe it was women. Women seemed to make men crazy. They always acted crazy around women until they got married. But the Old Man rarely brought women around to the trailer. It wasn't booze. He knew lots of drinkers. The trailer park was full of drinkers. The Old man would pull a quart of Gilbey's Gin from under the front seat of the car after work. He'd bolt down a good clear mouth full, breathing through his nose, and place the bottle back under the seat after carefully pulling the brown bag up around it again. There it stayed until the next afternoon.

Boy reached back into the far corner of the slim closet next to the bed. His hand felt the familiar .22 rifle, his tenth birthday gift. He pulled it out and caressed its smooth mahogany stock, opened and then threw the bolt. It made a satisfying lubricated machine sound as the hollow point bullet slid into the chamber. With his thumb, he flipped off the safety, revealing the red dot engraved into the breech, showing the rifle was ready to fire.

I could run away, he thought, but where to? He flicked the safety on and off with the tip of his finger. It clicked softly. I hate it here. He's getting too rough. I hurt. I don't want any more Sundays like this one. Not ever.

Setting the rifle butt on the floor, he reached down and slipped his right thumb through the guard and felt the trigger. He touched its familiar serrations gently. Opening his mouth, he took the small muzzle inside and tasted the acid steel with his tongue. He could taste the sweet oil, too. Even on this hot summer afternoon, the gun barrel felt cool. The front sight dug into the roof of his mouth. He had shot lots of groundhogs with this rifle, and he knew the meaty explosion that would happen when the bullet exploded his brain. It probably wouldn't come out. It was a small bullet. But if it did, it would make a bloody mess on the bed like strawberry jam. But the impact would snap his head back and throw his body down. Then his muscles would twitch, he knew that. He had seen it happen many times with dying groundhogs. Then he would pee. Groundhogs always peed when they died. A little trickle would always run down the side of the rock where they died.

The Old Man would be mad if he came home and the bed was a mess. He didn't like the bed to smell. He had taken several beatings for that.

The boy stood up and turned around, standing on the linoleum floor where the mess would be easier to clean up. Looking up, he caught himself in the closet mirror, the tear-stained face with a distorted mouth fit over the gun barrel like some dirty pencil drawing in the mens toilet. He looked at himself for several minutes. He thought about whether this would hurt or not. His thumb tightened, taking the slack out of the trigger mechanism, holding it tightly. He took a deep breath in through his nose and held it. And held it.

This is going to hurt, he thought.

A woman laughed lightly in the laundry room across the gravel drive.

He listened carefully but couldn't make out what the woman was saying. Most likely she was talking about her kids or her man. That's what women talked about doing laundry. Again, he held his breath and closed his eyes and tried to squeeze the trigger with his thumb. The thumb didn't seem to want to work. The oil started tasting bad. After long minutes he removed the gun barrel from his mouth.

"The hell with it," he said to himself. Racking the bolt, he ejected the bullet onto the floor, picked it up and fed it back into the magazine, closed the bolt on the empty chamber and carefully stood the thin little weapon back in the corner of the closet. I can always do this, he thought.

He dug around under the bed where the camping gear was kept and came up with a war surplus Marine pack. He threw a wadded shirt, a jacket, a pair of socks and his other set of underwear into it. Picking from the meager groceries, he placed two macaroni packages and an apple into the pack. He strapped the folding shovel on the back of the pack and found his sleeping bag and ground cloth and his web belt that held the military canteen with the olive-drab cover and the hunting knife in its leather sheath. After seasons of deer hunting in the mountains with the Old Man, he knew how to be comfortable. He often daydreamed of living alone in the outdoors, in the hills, in the trees by a running stream, and he carefully planned trips he'd never made, laying them out on maps, drawing routes in with crayon over the blue and black roads that twisted crazily through the mountains and canyons of western Colorado.

He dropped down to the outside trailer step and closed the door until the lock snapped. As he walked away from the road the Old Man used, he thought about where to go. Then he smiled. The adventure was upon him, owning his imagination. "Mountains! I'll go to the mountains!" Suddenly he felt better now that the adventure was set. It was nearly dark, the suns late glow sharply outlined the Front Range of the Rockies darkly purple against the red sky. The sun itself was a half-hour gone from the prairie.

As he came to the highway, he waited for a big diesel rig to growl past. He watched it roar by, watched it sight down the white line taking aim on the eastern horizon toward the Kansas wheat fields. He crossed the railroad tracks that carried the train to Chicago. After other whippings, he'd thought about catching it, but up close it always went by too fast, kicking up an explosion of dust and scattering bits of paper and weeds into the air. He had to turn his face away from the noise and flying trash.

Dropping down off the right-of-way, he was in a large field of weeds. There were no trees, but a half mile away were some grain elevators. On the opposite side of the field from the Chicago tracks were more train tracks, spurs for the grain storage. He had explored the open field as he had explored everything else around the trailer court and he had never seen anyone in the area between the two tracks. Walking into the middle of the field, he searched briefly and found what he was after. It was an irregular hole in the ground, as long as a man.

High weeds grew right up to the lip of the hole. In the last light, he took the folding shovel and began to dig, straightening the sides and leveling the bottom. When it was clean and level, he unrolled his ground cloth, spread it on the bottom, placed his sleeping bag inside and pulled the ground cloth over the top. He looked at the sky. It was clear. It wouldn't rain tonight. He was feeling better.

"Tired," he said, under his breath. He looked up over the edge of the hole, peering through the weeds in every direction. There was no movement out there. He dropped his head back and relaxed and looked at the night sky and his eyes closed. Tomorrow, he thought, I'll steal some money and hitchhike to the high country.

His sleep was fitful; he was hot then cold as his sweat cooled in the morning hours. He struggled through the nightmare he often had, a dream he couldn't remember completely in the morning, but it had to do with walking a narrow beam above giant steel gears, slowly rolling, shiny gears. A woman in a hat beckoned to him from the other side of the gear teeth. She was dressed in gray, clutching a large purse and she motioned slowly to him to come to her. He was afraid to walk over the threatening gears and afraid not to. He wanted to. He wanted to. He always wanted to.

He woke slowly, the sun in his eyes, baking in his sleeping bag. He thought about what would happen today. It wouldn't bring a thrashing from the Old Man. That was good. He was sore, and his head ached. He moved gingerly, yelping as the scabs rubbed and pulled the fabric of his shirt. He could hardly move his jaw.

"He does have one hell of a punch," he said to the weed field.

He covered the hole with the green ground cloth, putting rocks on each corner, and set off toward the grain elevators. A quick look showed there was nothing to steal from them but near a siding switch, he found a railroad signal lantern hanging on a post.

As the sun got higher, he decided to return to the hole for the day. The lantern, squat and heavy, was in good shape and he would use the lamp at night in the hole under the ground cloth so it couldn't be seen.

Back in the hole, he tried to think of a plan. He didn't have a cent. He lay in the sun on the sleeping bag trying to think of what to do. The mountains were a good place to go all right, but it would take some doing. He needed to get some money but the places he'd worked, the chicken hatchery and the bowling alley, would be the first places the Old Man would look. After sundown, he would forage for food.

Radishes and cabbages and some other vegetables he didn't know anything about grew in the truck farm next to the trailer court. The Shimodas owned it. The 'goddamjaps' the Old Man called them. He had fought on Peleliu and some other Pacific islands with the Marines, and he didn't have much truck with goddamjaps.

He moved carefully across the railroad, staying low out of the night sky. He waited until there were no cars and sprinted across the pavement to a thin stand of trees. He hunkered down in the trees and watched and listened, especially over toward the godamjaps' house. He felt good. He was the best at this. He always won at night games with the trailer court kids. He was the craftiest, the quietest. He breathed softly, controlling the sound of it, and listened carefully to the night sounds. There was no movement, only the gutty rasp of a diesel truck far off. He crouched and then scuttled into the vegetable field and dropped to the dirt between the rows. Lying on his side, he felt around for the small plants with the fat red roots. He grabbed a bunch low and pulled the radishes out with a soft tearing sound. The warm dirt smelled clean. He listened. Quiet. He crawled into the rows of cabbages.

"The goddamjaps are growin' me some good food," he whispered aloud. The cabbages were tall. Kneeling between the rows, he reached over into the spread leaves, found the solid center part of the head and with both hands, broke it off. It snapped louder than he expected. He dropped between the rows and held his breath. Suddenly, the fun was over. He was afraid. With short breaths he began to crawl between the rows, scrambling way from the goddamjaps' house, the cabbage tucked under his arm. A dog barked. He knew the dog. It was the goddamjaps' brown and white with the blue eye. He stopped. After a long time, the dog quit barking, and the boy scuttled toward the thin trees, spidery against the sky. He didn't stop at the trees but stood and began to trot. As he crossed in front of a storage building near the highway, he heard a car. It was near, nearer than it should be. He wheeled and began to run. Within a half dozen steps the car swung around the building and seized him up in two searing spotlights. He froze. The car slid to a stop, gravel flying up against the loading dock. It had lights on the top.

Doors on both sides flew open.

How did they find him? The boy looked around, but there was no place to run. He couldn't see against the spotlights. He looked down and shaded his eyes with his free hand. Sweat trickled down between his shoulder blades. The backs of his thighs felt funny. He didn't breathe. A shoe twisted in the gravel. The boy held the cabbage behind his back and waited, shaking, his blinded eyes wary and bright as a coyote's.

The sheriff walked up and grabbed him by the skinny arm, his voice was gentle, "Come on, son, get in th' car. We been lookin' fer yew."

Boy dropped the cabbage behind him. It rolled and lay on the ground like a new egg. His legs barely held him as he walked to the back door of the car, held open by the other sheriff.

The driver dropped heavily into the front seat and picked up the microphone. "Brighton One this is Brighton Three. We got this kid, and were bringin' him in."

"Okay, Brighton Three," the radio answered.

The patrol car rolled up to speed. "Boa, we been lookin' all over fer yew," the driver said, "Where yew been hidin' out, boa?"

"I don't know." He couldn't see their faces, but he felt they were smiling.

The rider turned, his arm crooked over the back of the seat.

"We're gonna take you up to the county jail for safe keepin'."

"By the way," The driver said over his shoulder, "Im Delbert, this is Bob. Yep, yo gonna be a jailbird tonight." The men laughed and watched a car go by fast, their heads turning exactly together. "Now that butthole is goin' way too fast…" Delbert said, "…but we ain't gonna pull 'im over now, we gotta get our desperate prisoner up ta th' slammer." They laughed again, easy laughs of men joking. The prisoner slumped back in the seat. He ran his hand over the back door looking for the handle. The handles and window cranks were gone, leaving only stubs sticking out.

The jail block was empty, and he was alone in the cell. By reaching high and hanging onto the bars, he could chin himself up and see some tree limbs and out onto a grassy place. The cell was empty except for a steel bunk hung on chains with a thin mattress. A metal sink and toilet without a seat hung on the wall. The walls were slick with dull green paint. Messages from former inmates were etched into the paint with thumbnails and little lines marked off days of boredom. A light bulb glowed from inside a metal cage high on the ceiling.

He sat on the bunk with his legs stretched out, and his head dropped back against the wall. He closed his eyes against the light. The mattress smelled like piss. How did they find me? He couldn't answer that one. They'll send me back to the Old Man, that's for sure. The Old Man will beat the hell out of me when I get back. He flexed his fingers, swollen from the wet washrag. Maybe they won't. Maybe they'll keep me here.

In the middle of the night, he woke up ravenous. He walked to the bars and yelled down the cell block into darkness. There was no answer. Stretching out again, he thought, boy, the Old Man's sure gonna to be mad as hell. It's gonna be rough.

Without opening his eyes, he woke at dawn with a great fear. What could he say to stop them from taking him home? He saw the anger in the Old Man's eyes, heard the sneering, biting words that tore at his insides, saw the start of punches so short and quick that he had never seen the end of one, only felt it. The blows to the solar plexus were bad. They took your breath away and made your back hurt from the inside. Or the nose. A shot to the nose makes you blind first because your eyes water, your stomach rolls over, and then you get dizzy. He imagined being quick enough to read where the blows were coming from, fast enough to get his elbows or forearms up, get his head tucked in behind his shoulder so the punch would slip off his shoulder, slide off his head and harmlessly away. That was hard since the Old Man was taller by a foot. Punching down had its advantages. Being able to punch at all had its advantages. He pondered the day when he would punch back; the Old Man would be surprised and mad, boring in with a savagery that scared him just thinking about it. No, he admitted to himself, he wouldn't swing back. It wasn't fair somehow. The Old Man was still the Old Man, and you damn well better not forget it.

A sheriff in a gray shirt and Levis appeared with a tin tray. He bent over and slid it through an opening in the bars near the floor. "Here ya go, young fella," he said pleasantly.

"When do I get out, sir?" the boy asked quietly.

"I don't know, soon mebbe." The sheriff left, closing the outside door behind him.

The prisoner fell on the food: oatmeal without salt, dry toast and black coffee. He left the coffee and ate the rest, picking up the toast crumbs off the steel tray with the tip of his finger and placing them carefully on his tongue.

In the late morning, the sheriff named Delbert opened the barred door.

"Well, lets go ole buddy, yo pa's waitin' fer ya."

"Yes, sir," he said softly.

During the half hour ride back to the trailer, Delbert talked every second, about his wife, about their new baby, about his new house. Occasionally he would hit the switch for the siren. As the turbine screamed up and down again, he would yell,

"Lookout, theres a cop aroun'," and he would laugh. The boy laughed, too. He wished he could laugh all day but laughing would be over soon. He could see the .22 rifle shining in the dark corner of the closet, feel its honest weight in his hands, see the magazine loaded with seven rounds, hear its bolt snick closed. Just like a groundhog...

The sheriff's car stopped behind the black Lincoln. The boy watched the trailer door crack open, and the Old Man fill it and step down.

Delbert got out. "Heres yore kid," he said cheerily, "He's 'n good shape and everythin'. He's ate breakfast this mornin', and we had a real nice visit." He ruffled the boys matted hair, one side of which swept upward. The Old Man flashed a smile, "Well, thanks for bringing him, I appreciate it."

"Yew bet, glad to hep out." Delbert turned and got into the white car. As he spun off in the gravel, he yelled, "Yew be good now and take good care of yo Pappy."

At the nod of the Old Man's head, the boy stepped up into the trailer. The Old Man followed and closed the door. The boy sat on the bed.

The Old Man sat on the couch and looked at him. "Well?" he said.

The boy shrugged, not looking up.

"You look at me when I speak to you."

He made himself look into the man's eyes and not flinch. "Yes, sir."

They watched each other quietly.

Finally, the Old Man spoke, "Don't you do that again. You worry everybody to death when you do things like that. I even called your aunt in California. She's worried sick."

There was another long silence. The boy forced himself to look into the face of his father. He felt the places his body hurt. He tried to force his swollen fingers to bend, but they resisted. Then the Old Man said, "Worried sick. I don't understand you. I've worked all my life for you, and you just can't do right can you?" His voice rose a notch, "Can you?"

"No, sir." He was motionless. Only the boys lips moved.

"Where were you all this time? Where in hell were you?"

"Out in the field across the tracks."

"Doing what for Christ sake?"

"Nothin'."

The Old Man stood and opened the door and spat tobacco juice outside. Then, "What's that on your pants?"

"Lamp oil."

"Well, don't get that crap on my bed. Take 'em off."

The boy moved tiredly.

"Hurry up, take 'em off, dammit. Move when I tell you to." His voice was raspy. "Go take a shower," he barked.

Quickly, the boy ran to the communal shower, relieved to be away from the trailer, and inside the damp room filled with the familiar earthy smells of the trailer court men. He showered, the water needling his raw skin. Dawdling, he listened to three truck drivers talking dirty about women they had known, each woman beautiful and ready to do sexy things to these rough men, willing so long as their husbands were away. He listened to them every chance he got. Their laughter rose and fell like someone playing with the volume knob of radio.

The boy had never been around women much. When he lived with his aunt, she paid attention to her son. They were Christian, so they never talked about such things. Even now he had no real clear idea what men and women did. He had grown up with men who talked dirty and was quite capable of talking dirty himself in the proper rhythms of a skillful curser. He usually did when out of reach of adults. His imagination was fired by the stories told by bricklayers about their women. The men spoke their secrets; shared their conquests while they hunched over the gray mortarboards or cold white bread lunches. The black hodcarriers had the best stories about jazz band dances and parking lot knife fights and young, hard-breasted black girls willing to do anything, whatever that meant. He had suspicions about what it meant, and they made him hard.

He could not remember being touched by a female except in passing, during the pursuits of checking ears or being corrected by a teacher. Sometimes, during night games with the kids in the trailer court, he could manage to brush up against smooth skin or graze a firm breast with his elbow. One night he had kissed a girl, her lips soft beyond soft. He liked the taste of her and savored it in his memory for weeks, but he couldn't imagine what it would be like to be around women all the time. Occasionally he would become the sympathetic target of a mother of one of the trailer camp kids. She would discover that he had no mother, nor had ever known one. She would cluck over his loss, and he would smile. He did not miss what he never had.

The Old Man was quiet for a month. Eating in silence, then going to work. Coming home, eating, going to bed after reading the paper. That suited the boy fine for there were no flying fists either. He worked, kept his nose clean, as the Old Man said and spoke only when spoken to.

It was Sunday when it finally broke. After the boy woke up, he went over to the bathroom. When he returned, he could tell it was going to be a long day. Sitting on the edge of the bed, the Old Man looked mad.

"Did you tell that Sheriff Delbert anything about me?"

"When?"

"When you were in Brighton, goddam it. Don't get smart with me."

"No, Sir. He didn't ask anything." Boy was wary now, his heart beating faster, calm on the outside but a hunted animal inside. He stared at the floor but concentrated on his side vision so that he might intercept, slip a punch, let it skip lightly off his face.

A snarl formed on the Old Man's face, rearranging it. "That Delbert, he's a shit-heel just like your mother's brothers. Trash. Goddam white trash. That's all he is, white trash." He paused, went to the front window and lifted the Venetian blind and looked out and around. It dropped like a guillotine. His voice was low. "What did you tell 'em about me? What? What?"

"Nuthin', I didn't tell em nuthin'." The boy said quietly, looking at the closed blind.

"You're lyin'. I know you're lyin'." The blocky man tugged on his belt buckle and the belt whistled through the pant loops The end fell limply to the floor, an extension of his muscular arm, the buckle tucked inside his knotted fist.

The boy held his breath but was relieved it wasn't the washrag. With the belt, he could cut his losses by half, at least. If the Old Man knew how much he feared the wash rag, he would certainly be using it now.

Boy was sharp now, watching the Old Man's eyes and the closed fist. The fist had to move first, but the eyes were the telegraph, the belt end would come a fraction of a second later. If one were quick, there was time to get an elbow or forearm or hand in the way to deflect, to break the unbroken arc, to change the rhythm of the swing, so it didn't hit flat and break the skin, burn like hot lime and bruise the muscle. But you had to be quick. The Old Man's eyes were dilated, nearly closing out the hazel iris.

"I'm going to teach you not to run off. White trash. You are a good-for-nothing, and you're not gonna buffalo me," he said under his breath. Swinging hard, the belt came in flat, the kid twisted on the balls of his feet, tucking an elbow tightly over his ribcage and, with his hand, caught the belt a hands length from the buckle, absorbing the rest on his lower back. As the strap recoiled, the old fighter whipped the belt into a backhanded serve, bringing it across his chest in a snap, the end curved away from the target, sprung with power. The boy cleanly missed with his hand, twisted the wrong way and caught the fully loaded leather strap across his shoulder blades. Like a spring, the power of the weapon was forced into its tip and, moving at a blur, collided with flesh with a dull thump. The impact rippled away in waves, forcing blood through cell walls, bursting capillaries and firing pain into the boy's brain. He was familiar with the delay between the actual strike and the pain flash but when it came, it was a sword thrust. He groaned from down in his throat, down in his chest, down in his gut.

He tracked the belt in the air, a black band wavering in his tears. Weakly, he put out his hand to break the arc, and he saw it serpent into his breast, biting into it and then releasing its fang, bringing skin with it. His breath left with a rush. His knees went weak and his anger rose, came up in his throat, choking him, into his watering eyes, blocking his breath and his reason. The vicious strap, a live thing, started back again. His timing was off. He was late, and he knew he had lost. He could only flail uselessly at the airborne weapon.

Then the boy surrendered. With a heave of his chest and an animal sound, he raised his head and faced the man squarely, staring into his wide eyes. The man stopped. There was a quiet final note in the boys voice. "I'll never cry for you again." It was a truth delivered. Slowly he placed hands on his head and presented his lean body to his father.

The Old Man's eyes flared with the challenge. He hissed, "I'll teach you to defy me. You won't defy me. Not for long." He swung the belt, wheeling with his full weight, using the power out of his legs and back, using his athletes timing and his anger to subdue the boy. Flexing in and out of a half crouch, he swung again and again. The kid watched the belt scythe in, shaped like an Arabic sword. He did not watch as his skin burst. At each strike, his breath drove out of him, and he inhaled between blows. Holding his hands on his head, he weaved with each impact. The tears flowed, but he made no sound.

After twenty manful swings, the Old Man stepped back, breathing hard, his eyes narrowed. He peered at the youth. His gaze fell over the skin running to red rivulets, the shape of the straps tip perfectly tattooed into the flesh, the patterns overprinted like a textile.

"That'll teach you," the Old Man muttered. As he went through the door, he snaked the belt back through the pants loops. "Worthless," he mumbled. The boy stood, weaving in the middle of the trailer, panting hard. He did not cry out.

Then he slept on the couch. During the night the welts bled and drained fluids and turned colors and formed scabs. He slept between a folded sheet, but there was no way to get comfortable. The sheet was a mess in the morning, stained red and yellow, soaked through and sticking to his skin and the couch upholstery. The Old Man went to work without breakfast and without speaking.

Boy felt weak like he was coming down with the flu. He spent the morning on the couch thinking, moving only when he had to. He thought about the rifle, but it had no appeal. There had to be a way out, a way to leave and avoid the sheriffs, a way to be gone and never face the Old Man again.

After last night, staying alive was not likely. Defying the Old Man like that, you just couldn't get away with it. Nobody could. The Old Man was the foreman of the bricklayers. He once fired a massive laborer called Double Ugly, and there had been a fight. Boy had watched. It was one good fight, too, as the brick foreman and the worker went after it on a new concrete floor with the reinforcing rods sticking up out of it. The big man would bore in, head down, roaring and cursing. The Old Man, some fifty pounds lighter, would sidestep him like a bullfighter and, as he went by, give him a shot to the cheekbone or the nose. The big man would go down hard on the raw floor. The Old Man would laugh at him and call him a pussy. Maddened, the big man would bull back into the fight and collect another shot. Finally, he didn't get up any more. He bled red splashes all over the white curing spray on the fresh concrete. Two other laborers helped him up and off the job. They said it took forty-six stitches to close the cuts on his jaw and around his eyes. "Your Dad is just a beautiful fighter," one of the bricklayers said, and that made the boy proud. No, this was the end of living with the Old Man for sure.

When the wind was right, Boy could hear the dogs yelping from the animal shelter a mile away. The small cinderblock building backed up to a narrow, dirty creek that turned green in the summertime. The dogs were kept in wire pens, and occasionally he would go look at them. He didn't want one; he would just watch, sometimes petting them through the wire. Other times he would tease them with a poking stick. Painted along the top of the building in big block letters was "American Humane Society."

As the boy shuffled into the office, a middle-aged woman looked over the top of her glasses at him. She was prim, with a big nose, and her shirt fit tight around her neck—it had little flowers on it. She smiled big, "May I help you, young man?"

"Maybe." The boy looked around the office. There were pictures of cats and dogs. He'd had a dog once, a golden cocker spaniel puppy, a gift from one of the Old Man's girlfriends. It lived for three weeks. One night it got real sick, crapped red all over the place and died. Distemper, somebody said. He felt sad, but it was no big deal.

"Yes?" The woman watched him, eyebrows up.

"Do you take care of hurt animals here?"

With a soft smile, she cocked her head. "Why yes, yes we do." She paused, then asked, "Do you have a hurt animal?"

"Yes, ma'am."

Her smile was genuine and motherly. "Aaaah. What kind of animal is it?" She put her elbows on the desk and leaned forward.

He took a deep breath. "It isn't an animal exactly." He looked away. "It's me. I need to get away from my old man."

The smile stayed, her voice was patient. "And what is the problem between you and your father?"

"He beats me up."

She smiled with understanding, "What do you mean beats you up? What do you do to deserve being treated like that?"

It was a trap. The boy knew it was a trap. He could get out of the trap by leaving. He could spring the trap by unbuttoning his shirt. All he wanted to do was leave the Old Man, not cause trouble. Boy sighed and started: "Ma'am, the Old Man beats me because he says I'm a shit-heel and a no-good. That's what he says. I don't know what I do...somethin' I guess...I don't know..." He shrugged.

The woman's smile faded. She turned stern. "We can't help people here, just animals. And don't talk like that, you're too young to talk like that. If you have some complaint like that you just have to speak to the police..." She looked down and began to move papers around on the desk. "I can't help you here."

The boy didn't move. There was a long silence except for the woman shuffling papers. She looked up, nearly angry.

"I tried that," he said, "They put me in jail and then they took me back to the Old Man. Nobody even talked to me."

She smiled and cocked her head. "Well now, they must have had good reason to take you back home. That's where boys your age belong." She smiled again, adjusting her glasses with her little finger pointing up into the air, "We all have disagreements with our parents from time to time. Where do you live?"

He nodded, "Over at the trailer court." Slowly, he began to unbutton his shirt from the top. He pulled it open.

"Oooh…" the woman said under her breath. "My God…" She stood quickly and turned away. She stared back sideways at his body. "Oh, my…" she said in a quivering voice.

It was quiet in the office. With a fluttery hand, she touched her hair and then walked around the desk. She was pale. With shaking hands, she held his shirt open. He could see the tears hanging in her eyes and smell a flowery perfume tinged with alcohol. She walked behind him, held his shirt away from his back nearly up over his head.

She sniffled. "Ohmygod…" she whispered. "Ohmygod…" She gently lowered his shirt without touching him. She walked back behind the desk without looking at him. He could barely hear her, "Would you come back in an hour or so. I'll need some time."

The boy went out behind the building and sat on the concrete steps. He never could tell where the Old Man might be. He didn't want to get caught here. He watched the dogs yip at each other, gossiping while waiting for adoption or death. Then he went back inside.

As if telling a secret, she whispers, "This afternoon at four o'clock you be out in front of the trailer court. A Reverend Johnson will pick you up and take you to his house. He'll take care of you, do you understand?"

"Yes, ma'am. Four o'clock."

Back at the trailer, he packed some clothes in a brown grocery bag. He wished he could take his rifle. I hate to leave my gun, he thought. I won't be coming back here, but I sure do hate to leave my gun. He left it standing in the back corner of the closet.

Alert for the Old Man's black Lincoln, he waited by the trailer court sign. A blue Plymouth coupe eased to a stop, and a graying man in a white collar with a friendly smile and a thin voice asked, "Are you the young man? From the animal shelter?"

"Yessir."

"Please get in, son."

The minister's house was cleaner than any house he had ever seen except for his grandmother's long ago. Grandma was very strict, and she smelled of snuff and old age and had once scolded him roundly for saying Darn. Grandpa was worse; humorless and unyielding, an utterly unforgiving Baptist preacher. The boy knew how to act around church people: talk clean, be polite, pray often and bathe regularly whether you wanted to or not.

The minister's wife clucked and fluttered around the guest room, laying out snowy white towels on the patchwork quilt. "Get out of those clothes; we'll wash 'em while you jump in th' shower."

He stood in the middle of the room and watched her fuss from chore to chore. He made no move to undress.

"Well, aren't you going to shower young man?"

"Yes, Ma'am," but he did not move.

"Well, they say you have been hurt. Let's have a look at you." The woman's fingers quickly slip the shirt's top button. His hand flies underneath her soft fingers and closes hard on the shirt, bunching it tightly in his fist.

The woman and the boy stand nose to nose. "Can't we just have a look?" she asks. "Perhaps we can clean the places, put something on them, so they'll feel better."

"No."

She looks into his face. Up close, the steeliness behind his soft brown eyes, a wild animal viciousness, take her aback. "Oh," she says, letting go. She steps back. "I'll just leave you alone. Come to the kitchen when you get cleaned up."

He stripped and showered. The water softened the scabs and hurt, but the air was sweet inside the steaming stall, not moldy like the trailer court. In dirty clothes, he sat at the dinner table. They said grace and the minister included him, "... and Lord Jesus, bless this child and protect him from harm and may you justly punish those responsible for his grievous injuries. In Jesus' name..." Together, they all said "...Amen." The only meal he could remember tasting as good was at Grandma's, years ago.

The clean sheets felt cool on his sores, even soothing. His scabs had almost stopped oozing, and he hoped they wouldn't dirty the sheets during the night. He thought about the Old Man. Damn, he sure as hell was going to be mad about this. The minister and his wife talked at the dinner table about going to court, whatever that meant, spoke of a foster home, talked about The Law. He thought about The Law and the dark jail and the oatmeal without salt and the sheriff playing with the siren and laughing and the trailer door opening and the Old Man's eyes. He saw the washrag slashing the air and the friendly .22 rifle standing in the closet and groundhog pee trickling down the side of a rock.

Easing down into the pristine whiteness, he thought about tomorrow. The Old Man would not stop searching for his property. The Old Man would find him here. Maybe not tomorrow, but soon. So tomorrow...he rolled his face into the fresh smelling pillow...tomorrow he would swipe some money and disappear into the high Rocky Mountains.

And never come back.

—END—

AFTERWORD

My life has been as much about luck as skill.

I was lucky that the book ideas cooked so long. It gave them time to mature.

I was lucky that I was of an age that kept me from writing into anger; lucky that I was married to Iris and that both she and my kids are so smart. Lucky that I was on an island in the Bahamas when the foolish idea of a book came out of the sky; that I wrote disastrously and that my next-door neighbor there was a very forgiving English teacher and encouraged me even though I had no idea what I was doing.

I am lucky that my memory cells still function, even if sporadically at this late date; that my friends have been bugging me to write for years; lucky that I have been healthy enough, and disagreeable enough to survive this long; lucky that I was born in America and proud of it even though it gets put down nowadays; lucky that clients hired me even though I was selling from an empty wagon; that after a dicey start, my life got good; that I lived wherever I wanted; worked when and wherever I wanted; made plenty of money, traveled the world, saw many things and did everything, came to understand somewhat the world and the people in it; lucky that people I didn't know were good to me and saved my life on several occasions; lucky to have consorted with only beautiful women; could see natural art before it became pictures on paper or canvas or movies; lucky that my photographer's eye allowed me to see deeper and more completely the beauty of the earth; lucky that my early days in business were catastrophic; that I took lessons away from these burning experiences that allowed me to be successful later when it was meaningful and the stakes were higher; lucky that I learned to teach and taught thousands of educated people how to communicate with strangers; lucky that they paid me well to do so and hired me again and again; lucky that people bought my books and learned from them; lucky that when life got tough I didn't know how to quit until the contest was over; lucky that I learned how to lose and then move on; lucky that I live in America, on the beach, that I lived in the exquisite High Rockies in the adventurous prime of my life; that I made lifetime friends that I hold dear.

This is a short list. I learned the difference between luck and skill. I learned that there are times when Dame Fortune reaches over the heads of a crowd of deserving, honest people and touches someone like me on the head. I can write pages on the subject of luck. This a very short list. The story, no matter how long or short, always ends with this: I was lucky to be lucky; I am the luckiest man I ever met.

Jerry Vass, 2017
Saint Augustine, Florida

THANKS

I am astounded at the good luck that brought me Marcella Hague, my beautiful editor, who single-handedly raised me up from the dark well of doubt about writing as an honorable activity and brought me into the bright daylight of confidence. She is a miraculous presence without whom this book would be just a series of 'Bubba' stories.

Iris, my lover of twenty-five years and my greatest stroke of luck, is the person who steadies my hand and checks my random and inaccurate navigation as I lurch through life, banging from one nutso idea to the next.

Belatedly, I want to thank my great friend of forty years, Genne Bowles, for all her gracious and enthusiastic support over the decades. She has a beautiful soul. She is irreplaceable.

VASS®
Publishing
1093 A1A Beach Blvd #448
Saint Augustine FL 32080
www.vass.com

Books by Jerry Vass

JUST MY LUCK
ISBN: 978-0-9629610-9-0

SLEEPING BIG IN SMALLVILLE
A Telluride Story
ISBN 978-0-9629610-5-2

SOFT SELLING IN A HARD WORLD
Plain talk on the Art of Persuasion
An Essential Handbook for Professionals and
Small Business Owners
2nd Edition Revised and Updated
80,000 in print
ISBN 978-076240401-8

SOFT SELLING TO EXECUTIVES
Plain Talk for Professionals
ISBN 978-096296107-6

All are available on amazon.com

Made in the USA
Columbia, SC
08 October 2017